RICK JAMES

JESUS
WITHOUT
RELIGION

What Did He Say? What Did He Do?  What's the Point?

IVP Books

An imprint of InterVarsity Press
Downers Grove, Illinois

Downers Grove, Illinois InterVarsity Press
P.O. Box 1400, Downers Grove, IL 60515-1426
World Wide Web: www.ivpress.com
E-mail: email@ivpress.com

InterVarsity Press® is the book-publishing division of InterVarsity Christian Fellowship/USA®, a student movement active on campus at hundreds of universities, colleges and schools of nursing in the United States of America, and a member movement of the International Fellowship of Evangelical Students. For information about local and regional activities, write Public Relations Dept., InterVarsity Christian Fellowship/USA, 6400 Schroeder Rd., P.O. Box 7895, Madison, WI 53707-7895, or visit the IVCF website at <www.intervarsity.org>.

Design: Cindy Kiple
Images: Radius/PunchStock

ISBN 978-0-8308-3607-9

Printed in the United States of America ∞

Library of Congress Cataloging-in-Publication Data

James, Rick, 1963-
  Jesus without religion: what did He say? what did He do? what's the
  point?/by Rick James.
    p. cm
  Includes bibliographical references.
  ISBN-13: 978-0-8308-3607-9 (pbk.: alk. paper)
  1. Jesus Christ—Biography. I. Title.
  BT301.3.J36 2007
  232.9'01,dc22
  [B]

                                  2007016682

| P | 18 | 17 | 16 | 15 | 14 | 13 | 12 | 11 | 10 | 9 | 8 | 7 | 6 | 5 | 4 | 3 |
| Y | 22 | 21 | 20 | 19 | 18 | 17 | 16 | 15 | 14 | 13 | 12 | 11 | 10 | 09 | | |

Dedicated to Mary Kate James

CONTENTS

PREFACE

I think at some point just about everyone takes a run at reading the Bible. People turn to it for comfort, direction, security, to ward off evil, for answers to their obsessing questions (*Will I ever get married? Will I die in a disfiguring accident? Am I unknowingly a Judas . . . the Antichrist?*). But most often the motive for turning to the Bible is simply a desire to understand—or perhaps "figure out"— Jesus.

You can live on the hands of Jesus Standard (or "A.D.") Time for only so long before experiencing some curiosity about who Jesus is. So we turn to the Bible—more specifically, the Gospels—to discover Jesus. But it isn't long before the culture, language, genre and historical context of the thing grind our exploration to a halt. The person of Jesus remains uncharted territory, simply the etched contour of an enormous landmass, with a cross scribbled somewhere in the interior. We can get the sense that the real message and meaning of the Gospels—and of Jesus—is out of reach, reserved for Bible scholars and theologians: those with pointy heads and pointy beards.

I don't believe this to be the case. In fact I know this is not the case. The problem isn't that the Bible, the Gospels or Jesus are too esoteric or ethereal. It's that we attempt to understand them without any context whatsoever—which is rather silly, if you think about it. If you don't know the context, even the back of a cereal box is cryptic and enigmatic: cartoons that aren't funny, games that aren't entertaining, club memberships and offers that no one will ever respond to. If I handed you a cereal box and told you it was a newspaper, you'd think the world had come unscrewed. It's not meant to be engaging; it's meant to be something you stare at while you eat your breakfast and attempt to wake up. Context is everything.

The Bible, I believe, is a divinely inspired book. But therein lies the rub. It is an inspired *book,* not a fortune cookie. So if we go jumping into the middle (where the Gospels are, where Jesus is) without any context, it's going to create some serious comprehension problems.

In my Bible the Gospels begin on page 807. There aren't a lot of books you can jump into on page 807 and not have missed much (with the possible exception of *Moby Dick*). It's a little like trying to figure out the movie plot simply from scene selections 18-22—it ain't gonna happen. To get the whole story, you have to get the whole story. A lot of questions about Jesus are answered by understanding the entire plot: how the Gospels and Jesus intersect with the history and story of the Old Testament that precedes it.

And then there's the context of genre. As Jesus so un-succinctly puts it in Mark 4:22, "Whatever is hidden is meant to be disclosed, and whatever is concealed is meant to be brought out into the open." If you can believe it, Jesus said this to clarify why his lessons were so confusing, because a lot of his teaching was done in the form of parables (something like fables, with a spiritual message embedded in the story) and proverbs. If you can recognize the genre of a book or passage you've gone a long way to figuring out its meaning.

A third context is culture. In Matthew 23:25 Jesus says, "Woe to you, teachers of the law and Pharisees, you hypocrites! You clean the outside of the cup and dish, but inside they are full of greed and self-indulgence." If you don't know that the Pharisees were consumed with ritualistic purity like cleaning cups and utensils, I'm not sure how you'd take this statement—Jesus hates dishwashers? But the message behind the statement is that the Pharisees were focused on externals and ignoring internal corruption. The people listening to Jesus would have nodded their heads, perhaps even snickered a bit. Without that cultural context, however, cooks, dishwashers and perhaps the whole restaurant industry—according to the Bible—are headed to hell in handbaskets, or doggybags as the case may be.

Finally, the Gospels are themselves stories. True, they are history, but like a History Channel documentary on the Olsen Twins, which moves from the *Full House* years to the WalMart clothing line, the material in each of the Gospels has been thoughtfully arranged to bring out themes and flow from a beginning to an end. So, for example, Matthew begins his story with Jesus' family tree, while Mark begins his story with Jesus' cousin John, and both of them do so for a reason.

Now, I could add other contexts—like, for example, how someone decides to translate a particular passage in the Bible from its original language—but these four will go a long way toward unlocking meaning. And the good news is that I'm going to explore these contexts for you. You should be able to read this book in one sitting and afterward have a solid grasp of the basic flow, context and meaning of who Jesus was, what he said, and what he did.

This book's structure follows the basic structure of the Gospels. The Gospels, taken together, tell the story of Jesus: from the unique series of events surrounding his birth, through the three years of his public ministry (recounting his teachings and miracles), to his final trip to Jerusalem and, day by day, the last week of his life: his betrayal, death and resurrection.

But I shall not leave you there orphaned. By the end of the book we'll know each other well enough to dispense with politeness and talk honestly about implications. I'll try to put everything you've read, and I've written, into some broader perspective, something that makes sense.

As this is religious subject matter, I feel I should give a disclaimer up front. I write with considerable bluntness, and generally, if it pops into my mind, it appears on paper. I, of course, could edit myself, but for the most part I choose not to because I'd like this book to be as accessible and down-to-earth as possible, as such subject matter rarely is. But I do want to say that it is neither my desire nor my goal to be irreverent, only relatable. And don't mistake my manner of communication for either apathy or agnosticism—I assure you I'm neither.

Rather through context, commentary and considerable bluntness, my desire is to strip away the veneers of both religiosity and skepticism (which has its own creeds) and get down to the bare wood, looking to arrive at not some austere set of facts but the unvarnished Jesus of the Gospels and history—Jesus without religion.

1   CONTACT

Jesus Arrives on Planet Earth

Once upon a time . . .

> There was a wise man who was called Jesus, and his conduct was
> good, and he was known to be virtuous. And many people from
> among the Jews and the other nations became his disciples. Pilate
> condemned him to be crucified and to die. And those who had be-
> come his disciples did not abandon their loyalty to him. They re-
> ported that he had appeared to them three days after his
> crucifixion, and that he was alive. Accordingly they believed that
> he was the Messiah, concerning whom the Prophets have re-
> counted wonders.[1]

With phrases such as "his conduct was good" and "he was known to be
virtuous," you may have thought that Jane Austen wrote the above description of Jesus, but it was actually written by Flavius Josephus, born
in A.D. 37, only a few years after the death of Jesus (around A.D. 30–33).
We begin here—not with Matthew, Mark, Luke or John—as a reminder
that in the Gospels we will be retracing concrete historical events, not
vague religious ones. As Josephus attests, these things really happened.

Though every Easter *Time* or *Newsweek* or some other popular mag-
azine goes in search of the historical Jesus, their quest is driven more by
circulation numbers than finding answers. The resulting articles are
more in the genre of entertainment than scholarship, with the most po-

larizing or radical views being thrown together in a ring. This is not to say that there isn't legitimate debate about who Jesus was, nor that certain events don't require the acquiescence of faith, but the fact is that there *is* considerable scholarly consensus on the historical Jesus.

The problem, of course, is that consensus doesn't make a good cover story: "What We've Always Thought About Jesus Is Pretty Much True" isn't likely to move many magazines. And so facts not withstanding, every Easter we will continue to read that "new findings" have placed "everything we ever thought" "under siege" and that "scholars" are locked in a "battle for the Bible" and "quest" for the "historical Jesus." This year, we will no doubt "uncover," that Jesus was actually a Viking explorer with a really bad sense of direction.

But the accuracy of the Gospel's birth accounts has been established by the most stringent of historical and social apparatuses: gossip. Jesus and Christianity had their share of enemies, and several of the Gospels circulated within Israel shortly after his death. If anyone had stepped forward and said, "That's a bunch of לְתרהרְכָ [for authenticity, I've left the Hebrew untranslated]. Jesus was a falafel vendor outside of Jericho," Christianity would have withered and died. But they didn't, so it didn't. Rather, Christianity spread like pollen, because give or take a virgin birth or resurrection (issues requiring faith), there was consensus within Israel upon the basic facts as described in the Gospels.

John began his Gospel by connecting Jesus directly to God:

> In the beginning was the Word, and the Word was with God, and the Word was God. He was with God in the beginning. . . .
> The Word became flesh and made his dwelling among us. (John 1:1, 2, 14)

Mark's Gospel begins with Jesus as an adult and leads with his cousin John:

The beginning of the gospel about Jesus Christ, the Son of God.

It is written in Isaiah the prophet:

"I will send my messenger ahead of you." . . .

And so John came, baptizing in the desert. (Mark 1:1, 2, 4)

So we're left with only Matthew and Luke to compile a scrapbook of the events surrounding Jesus' birth. If you were curious about issues of teething, bedtimes, allowances or how many hours Mary was in labor, I'm afraid you're out of luck. The Gospel writers included only those events having special significance to Jesus' identity and future ministry. This is a common practice for all stories, fact or fiction: the story of Batman, for example, is compelling even though it doesn't include his first steps or first day of school, but it would be unintelligible without the death of his parents or his encounter with a cave full of bats. So the Gospels contain only a handful of stories about his childhood, yet each will prove foundational to understanding Jesus.

Virgin Born

This is how the birth of Jesus Christ came about: His mother Mary was pledged to be married to Joseph, but before they came together, she was found to be with child through the Holy Spirit. Because Joseph her husband was a righteous man and did not want to expose her to public disgrace, he had in mind to divorce her quietly.

But after he had considered this, an angel of the Lord appeared to him in a dream and said, "Joseph son of David, do not be afraid to take Mary home as your wife, because what is conceived in her is from the Holy Spirit. She will give birth to a son, and you are to give him the name Jesus, because he will save his people from their sins."

All this took place to fulfill what the Lord had said through the prophet: "The virgin will be with child and will give birth to a son, and they will call him Immanuel"—which means, "God with us." (Matthew 1:18-23)

Television journalist Larry King was once asked who, from all of history, he would like to interview. He immediately answered, "Jesus Christ." Then he added what his first question would be: " 'Are you indeed virgin born?' . . . The answer to that question would explain history for me."[2] Perhaps I lack the spiritual depth of Larry King, but the first question on my list would probably be more along the line of, "Whatever happened to my old dog, Banjo?" The question of the virgin birth would certainly be in my top ten, though, because the answer would explain a lot.

Matthew begins his account with the words, "This is how the birth of Jesus Christ came about." Matthew is not introducing his audience— Jews living in Israel only decades after the death of Jesus—to a new story but filling in details of a story they already know: setting the record straight, clearing up any misconceptions, rumors or hearsay. A virgin birth would generate plenty of gossip, and Matthew must rescue the historical facts from both skeptics and well-meaning believers who might exaggerate and overspiritualize them—"The way I heard it, Mary gave birth to a 30-year-old man named Jesus, beard and all." This, according to Matthew, is how the birth of Jesus *really* happened.

Mary was "pledged to be married to Joseph" (verse 18), which in Israel was more of a quasi wedding than a quasi engagement. You were essentially married, only not yet living together, giving you all of the monogamy with none of the fringe benefits, and, I suppose, making it all the more difficult for Joseph to digest the news that Mary was pregnant. Mary's pregnancy would have created a nasty scandal, and rather than expose her to public shame and possible execution, Joseph graciously decided on a quiet divorce—until, Matthew tells us, Joseph had a dream. In fact, it must have been quite a dream, for this is probably not the first time in the history of unplanned pregnancies that someone claimed "miraculous conception," but undoubtedly it is the first time someone believed it.

One would assume that being the parents of the Messiah would guarantee certain privileges with God, but in the Gospels, divine communication with Mary and Joseph is always mediated indirectly through angels or dreams. This unexpected detail may have been simply Matthew setting the record straight, or perhaps the detail itself is pregnant with the seed of Jesus' message: even the best of the human species stand at a distance from the Creator, and need a mediator to bridge the gulf. In either case it affirms what most of us intuit to be true about the universe: there are worlds well beyond our windows.

The most persuasive evidence for the claim of Jesus' virgin birth hinges on a sign contained within the book of Isaiah: a book written roughly seven hundred years before Jesus was even born. The prophet Isaiah made the following prediction: "The Lord himself will give you a sign: The virgin will be with child and will give birth to a son, and will call him Immanuel" (Isaiah 7:14). Isaiah goes on to describe the miraculous child:

He will be called
    Wonderful Counselor, Mighty God,
    Everlasting Father, Prince of Peace.
Of the increase of his government and peace
    there will be no end.
He will reign on David's throne
    and over his kingdom,

establishing and upholding it
with justice and righteousness
from that time on and forever. (Isaiah 9:6, 7)

The virgin birth, then, is not simply a miracle or some bizarre happenstance, but more significantly, it was the agreed-upon sign between God and his covenant people, Israel, indicating that the Deliverer had arrived.

What exactly is a sign? *The Oxford English Dictionary* defines *sign* as "an indication, pointer, signal or evidence of what is happening or going to happen." *Oxford* also declares a sign to be "any trace of a wild animal, especially its tracks or droppings." Clearly irrelevant, but you have to admire the forward-thinking Oxford editors for including animal droppings in their definition.

Now, in the long history of human egos many have aspired to be the Messiah. Whether they wanted to fool people into following them or they were themselves convinced they were the Messiah (asylums are full of the latter), there has been no shortage of imposters. So, through the prophet Isaiah, God's people were promised a sign (a pointer, a signal, evidence) that God would, in fact, be with us. That sign was to be a virgin bearing a child, and the Gospel writer did not want us to miss the fact that Jesus was born of a virgin. Then again, maybe it was more than just a sign; maybe it was also a necessity. Maybe the double helix of human DNA is more twisted than we thought, such that it can't produce a sinless Messiah any more then it could produce a llama. I mean, even the greatest recipe, if it contained dirt, would create the greatest meal—containing dirt.

And yet a sign, even a miraculous sign, can be rationalized and dismissed without faith. Even with all our science and intellectual posturing, we still believe what we want to believe. So it's not surprising that in some of the Jewish literature opposing Christianity in its early centuries, Jesus is referred to as "a bastard son of an adulteress."[3] But this only confirms a historical consensus on the main fact—Mary was pregnant apart from Joseph.

The virgin birth was the first sign that Jesus was no ordinary child. But other indicators were to follow.

Bethlehem: A Way in a Manger

After Jesus was born in Bethlehem in Judea, during the time of King Herod, Magi from the east came to Jerusalem and asked, "Where is the one who has been born king of the Jews? We saw his star in the east and have come to worship him."

When King Herod heard this he was disturbed, and all Jerusalem with him. When he had called together all the people's chief priests and teachers of the law, he asked them where the Christ was to be born. "In Bethlehem in Judea," they replied, "for this is what the prophet has written:

"'But you, Bethlehem, in the land of Judah,
   are by no means least among the rulers of Judah;
for out of you will come a ruler
   who will be the shepherd of my people Israel.'"

Then Herod called the Magi secretly and found out from them the exact time the star had appeared. He sent them to Bethlehem and said, "Go and make a careful search for the child. As soon as you find him, report to me, so that I too may go and worship him." (Matthew 2:1-8)

Let's begin with the most obvious question: What's a Magi? Simple: in order to rule efficiently, kings needed a cabinet of counselors—wise men. In the ancient world, part of what made a wise man wise was the ability to determine the currents of the future through the charting of stars and constellations. So, in context, "Magi" refers to those individuals who were at the same time royal cabinet members, counselors and astronomers, sent as ambassadors of good will from other nations.

At first glance the visit of the Magi has a bit of a tall tale feel to it, but that has less to do with history and more to do with bizarre crèche displays we see on people's lawns at Christmas? (Wise men, sheep, camels, cows, angels: why not throw in a statue of Karl Marx for good measure?) In fact the Roman historian Suetonius (A.D. 70-130) mentions just such a delegation of Magi arriving in Rome in A.D. 66 to pay homage to Nero. Both Suetonius and Tacitus (A.D. 56-117) also tell us that at the turn of the era there was an expectation that a world ruler would come from Judea (Israel), so there is nothing strange about an entourage of Magi arriving in Israel—perhaps it would have been strange if they had not.[4]

The Magi came to Herod, the Jewish king, whom they naturally assumed would be aware of a new king's birth taking place within his own country. He wasn't. Herod didn't stay current on such spiritual matters and had to ask his own wise men, the "chief priests and teachers of the law," what the Scriptures said about the location of the Messiah's birth. The answer: Bethlehem.

The modern city of Bethlehem is about as remarkable as Cleveland. There's no telling where tax and tourist dollars have been squandered, but then again, I wouldn't know how much it costs to keep a three-thousand-year-old city from sifting into sand. The ancient city of Bethlehem was—I dare say—even less remarkable, and yet the Jewish scholars and "teachers of the law" knew that this would be the address of the Messiah, and here is why they knew. The prophet Micah made a pronouncement—on God's behalf—that the Messiah would be born in the city of Bethlehem. This prediction, dated roughly 750 years before the birth of Jesus, reads as follows:

You, Bethlehem Ephrathah,

though you are small among the clans of Judah,

out of you will come for me

one who will be ruler over Israel,

whose origins are from of old,

from ancient times. (Micah 5:2)

You have to admit, that's pretty amazing. About the only thing that could possibly blunt the impact of this prediction is the ill-conceived notion that such ancient prophecies were ubiquitous, with seers spouting oracles on every street corner of the ancient world. In *Star Wars* there is a foretelling of one who would bring balance to the Force. The Lord of the Rings is saturated with messianic language. And while I apologize for mentioning this movie in the same breath, in *The Chronicles of Riddick* Vin Diesel plays the Furion, prophesied to level an empire. And what about the medieval mystic Nostradamus? Here, for example, is one of his most famous prophecies:

Takes the Goddess of the Moon, for his Day & Movement:

A frantic wanderer and witness of God's Law,

In awakening the world's great regions to Gods will.[5]

This is said to be a reference to the late Princess Diana. I know, a shock to me too, as I thought it sounded eerily like Martha Stewart. And that's just it: the prophecy is so vague it could be about anyone. Truth be told, academic testing of predictions by the world's most renowned psychics yielded a success rate of roughly 11 percent, which might not be so dismal if the control group, making random guesses concerning the future, didn't score at the same 11 percent rate of accuracy. (I'm sure the psychics scored much higher on bending spoons and giving dating advice.)

In contrast, biblical prophecies almost always contain a clear and verifiable predictive element. Amidst the imagery and poetics are predictions as tangible as a piece of produce; they can be sniffed, squeezed and weighed for accuracy. This is not "When the lima bean weeps, the trolls of perdition shall promenade to sounds of salsa and laughter" kind of nonsense. This is a statement of future fact: "The Messiah will be born in the town of Bethlehem."

Furthermore, the prophets whose messages were preserved as Scripture were included there because of their flawless prophetic accuracy during their own lifetime. If they said it, it had come to pass. And on that reputation, their predictions concerning the far future—those that went beyond their lifetime—were anticipated with confidence.

To all of this, Judaism added a final layer of quality control. If someone claiming to be a prophet made a prediction that didn't come to pass, the law required that they be executed—an ingenious method for weeding out prophetic mediocrity.

The Old Testament contains sixty-one specific prophecies and nearly three hundred references to the future Messiah. The Gospel writers wanted their audience to realize that Jesus had fulfilled (or would fulfill) every last one of them. But for a second, let's forget about the other 299 and just think about this one: if we can safely rule out both Princess Diana and Martha Stewart, how many people in human history who could remotely qualify for the title of Messiah were born in Bethlehem? Not a lot of names come back based on that search query. And yet Jesus was born there—what are the odds?

"What are the odds?" is, of course, just a figure of speech. But if you would in fact like to know the odds, mathematics professor Peter Stoner worked up the numbers. He calculated the odds against one person fulfilling just eight of the sixty-one specific prophecies at 1 in 10^{21}. To illustrate that number, Stoner gave the following example: "First, blanket the entire Earth land mass with silver dollars 120 feet high. Second, specially mark one of those dollars and randomly bury it. Third, ask a person to travel the Earth and select the marked dollar, while blindfolded, from the trillions of other dollars."[6]

While I'm sure that was protractor-gripping amusement for math and physics majors, I promise that was the last time we'll be doing math. To summarize, then, Jesus' birth in Bethlehem was the second major messianic sign. That's being born of a virgin + being born in Bethlehem = two signs.

Oops, more math. Sorry, forgot. I also forgot, or nearly did, that there is a fuller discussion on the features of messianic prophecy found in the appendix, should you want to be briefed on it.

The Census: God and Governments

In those days Caesar Augustus issued a decree that a census should be taken of the entire Roman world. (This was the first census that took place while Quirinius was governor of Syria.) And everyone went to his own town to register.

So Joseph also went up from the town of Nazareth in Galilee to Judea, to Bethlehem the town of David, because he belonged to the house and line of David. He went there to register with Mary, who was pledged to be married to him and was expecting a child. While they were there, the time came for the baby to be born, and she gave birth to her firstborn, a son. She wrapped him in cloths and placed him in a manger, because there was no room for them in the inn.

And there were shepherds living out in the fields nearby, keeping watch over their flocks at night. An angel of the Lord appeared to them, and the glory of the Lord shone around them, and they were terrified. But the angel said to them, "Do not be afraid. I bring you good news of great joy that will be for all the people. Today in the town of David a Savior has been born to you; he is Christ the Lord. This will be a sign to you: You will find a baby wrapped in cloths and lying in a manger." (Luke 2:1-12)

I've known for quite some time that Santa isn't real. The day my parents told my older brother the truth about Santa was the same day he told me. And hopefully it won't come as a shock to you, but very few of our Christmas holiday traditions have their roots in the Gospels. Rudolph, Frosty, mistletoe, Christmas trees: the Gospels have none of it. These are gritty accounts, unsanitary times, life without anesthetic.

People must always be counted because people must always be taxed. Roman sources suggest that Caesar's census did in fact take place but locate it in the springtime and not winter, which leads to the obvious question: "Why is Christmas celebrated in December, instead of closer on the calendar to, say, opening day of trout season (April 15)?" I know this is a detour, but I think it's a detour worth taking. So we're taking it—all the way to Mardi Gras.

Mardi Gras is part cultural mosaic and part cultural train wreck: at times an artful blending of cultures and at other times, well, a bloody head-on collision. In browsing the folk art and voodoo shops of Bourbon Street in New Orleans, you'll witness one of those collisions. Amid the assorted deities, dolls and devils, you'll find the Virgin Mary hiding, as though embarrassed to be present. What's the Virgin Mary doing in a voodoo shop? How did it come to this?

This is commonly called Christianization. It is what happens when a culture absorbs Christian ideas but the overarching belief structure never changes. Up until the fourth century A.D., the Roman empire was largely antagonistic toward Christianity: at best, Christians were tolerated, at worst, they were martyred in the coliseum. But when the emperor Constantine was converted to Christianity, instead of simply purchasing a Bible or getting a Jesus fish for his chariot, he decided to legislate Christianity onto his empire. But true Christian faith can never be legislated, and Constantine had to settle for Christianizing the populace. It's probable he accomplished this, among other shrewd political choices, by changing the end-of-year pagan festivities (winter solstice) into Christmas, since even for a dictator, expunging a national holiday can be political suicide. The ensuing centuries abound with many such compromises, some violent and inhumane, and it could be argued that Christianity was better off under persecution than suffering this corrosive marriage with the culture. (Then again, I'm not next in line to wrestle a lion in the coliseum, so I'll keep my opinion to myself.)

So just as it would be a terrible miscalculation to assume that Urban Outfitters is a Christian company because it sells Jesus figurines and "Jesus is my homeboy" T-shirts, it would also be wrong to assume that everything that has gone on in history under the name of Christianity is an expression of sincere Christian faith. It simply isn't. We never seem to get to the real Jesus when all we talk about is the behavior of people while wearing a cross, because anyone can wear a cross—and wearing a cross doesn't prevent us from doing anything. In fact, if I were the Satan, I think I'd wear one whenever I went out in public—it goes good with black.

With that detour out of the way, let's get back to the unsanitized, demythologized, not-fit-for-Hallmark version of Christmas that we find in the Gospels: Forced to enroll in a Roman census, amid stinging rumors of infidelity and promiscuity, a sixteen- or seventeen-year-old girl named Mary rode twenty-six miles to Bethlehem on the back of a donkey—in her third trimester. (While statues depict the blue-clad Mary with her heart visibly radiating from her sternum, we should presume that she made the journey with her heart beating safely within her rib cage.) Upon arrival, there were no vacancies, and so Mary enjoyed the further blessing of birth labor from the vantage point of a stable floor (probably belonging to Joseph's family). Perhaps this was God's plan, or perhaps Joseph—failing to plan—arrived late. But we are left viewing irony itself: the Messiah entered the world, only to land in an animal's feeding trough, because nobody had any room for him.

The Wonder Years

When Joseph and Mary had done everything required by the law of the Lord, they returned to Galilee to their own town of Nazareth. And the child grew and became strong; he was filled with wisdom, and the grace of God was upon him.

Every year his parents went to Jerusalem for the Feast of the Passover. When he was twelve years old, they went up to the Feast, according to the custom. After the Feast was over, while his parents were returning home, the boy Jesus stayed behind in Jerusalem, but they were unaware of it. Thinking he was in their company, they traveled on for a day. Then they began looking for him among their relatives and friends. When they did not find him, they went back to Jerusalem to look for him. After three days they found him in the temple courts, sitting among the teachers, listening to them and asking them questions. Everyone who heard him was amazed at his understanding and his answers. When his parents saw him, they were astonished. His mother said to him, "Son, why have you treated us like this? Your father and I have been anxiously searching for you."

"Why were you searching for me?" he asked. "Didn't you know I had to be in my Father's house?" But they did not understand what he was saying to them.

Then he went down to Nazareth with them and was obedient to

them. But his mother treasured all these things in her heart. (Luke 2:39-51)

The childhood years of Jesus truly are the "wonder years," for we are left to wonder where in the world he wandered off to. While the Gospels contain intricate details of Jesus' adulthood, Luke alone provides us with this one story from his adolescence. That's it: just a handful of sentences, but enough to partially answer the question we always inquire of greatness: When did they know they were different?

As his later book of Acts and the writings of early leaders of the church attest, Luke's research for his Gospel included firsthand interviews with some of the disciples. This story from Jesus' adolescence, along with phrases such as "Mary treasured up all these things and pondered them in her heart" (Luke 2:19) and other details in the Gospel, led many to speculate that Mary, the mother of Jesus, was among those whom Luke interviewed. While this is speculative, I'm very fond of speculation.

In some ways the snapshot contained in this passage is almost comical, for while Mary and Joseph are universally upheld as the models of parenthood, in the one story we have of Jesus' adolescence, he went missing for an entire day—and nobody noticed. I think today this would earn a visit from Child Protection Services. The likely explanation, however, is that the entire extended family traveled together, and it was simply assumed that Jesus was with other family members. Whatever their anxieties might have been, Mary and Joseph trace Jesus back to Jerusalem and ultimately to the Temple, where they find him riddling the religious leaders with questions. What we need to know of Jesus' adolescence, according to the need-to-know sensibilities of the Gospel writers, is this: by the age of twelve, Jesus appears to be aware of who he is and what he has come to do.

It is not surprising or problematic that the Gospel writers would want to devote the majority of their Gospels to Jesus' ministry years, but it became a problem a century later, when this hole in Jesus' biography was spackled by a series of accounts written under the pseudonyms of apostles (The Gospel of Thomas, The Gospel of Judas, etc.). Like an episode of *Smallville* chronicling the exploits of a teenage Clark Kent, these gospels attribute all sorts of adolescent shenanigans to Jesus. This is my favorite from the Infancy Gospel of Thomas.

> The son of Annas the scribe was standing there with Jesus. Taking a branch from a willow tree, he dispersed the puddle of water, which Jesus had gathered. When Jesus saw what had happened, he became angry and said to him, "You godless, brainless moron, what did the ponds and waters do to you? Watch this now: you are going to dry up like a tree and you will never produce leaves or roots or fruit." And immediately, this child withered up completely.[7]

The moral of this story: don't mess with Jesus' puddle—ever. But far from being harmless novels, most of these stories were actually propaganda for a cult of the second and third centuries, known as Gnosticism. Holding to the belief that the physical world (as opposed to the spiritual world) and our physical bodies were evil, the Gnostic cult behind the Gospel of Thomas struggled not with the deity of Jesus but with the idea that God would take on evil, corrupt flesh. In other words, their raging doubt was not whether Jesus was the unique Son of God, but whether Jesus was truly a man.

Early leaders of the church were aware of such writings as the Gospel of Thomas and the Gospel of Judas, taking them only as serious as to list them among the newest works of fiction (dating at least a hundred years after the original Gospels), and warn of their veiled attempt to strip Jesus of his humanity. The Christian leader Irenaeus (A.D. 120–190) wrote authoritatively: "There are four gospels and only four, neither more nor less: four like the points of the compass, four like the chief directions of the wind."[8]

These Gnostic gospels still have historical interest (at least I find them interesting), but clearly they are not Scripture. Which perhaps raises in your mind some broader questions concerning the New Testament. You might want to pause for a few answers, found in appendix A, before moving on. Otherwise we'll jump ahead, through the next eighteen years, to the beginning of Jesus' public ministry.

John the Baptizer

The beginning of the gospel about Jesus Christ, the Son of God.

It is written in Isaiah the prophet:
> "I will send my messenger ahead of you,
>   who will prepare your way"—
> "a voice of one calling in the desert,
> 'Prepare the way for the Lord,
>   make straight paths for him.'"

And so John came, baptizing in the desert region and preaching a baptism of repentance for the forgiveness of sins. The whole Judean countryside and all the people of Jerusalem went out to him. Confessing their sins, they were baptized by him in the Jordan River. John wore clothing made of camel's hair, with a leather belt around his waist, and he ate locusts and wild honey. And this was his message: "After me will come one more powerful than I, the thongs of whose sandals I am not worthy to stoop down and untie. I baptize you with water, but he will baptize you with the Holy Spirit." (Mark 1:1-8)

Like everyone with a digital camera I take a ton of photos, never printing any of them. I was recently looking at an amazing shot of my wife and me, taken in the center of Teatralny Square in Warsaw, Poland. Well, that's not really true. It's a great shot of the Square, but objectively speaking, it looks like a movie poster for *Dawn of the Dead.* I didn't see them at the time, and have no idea who they are, but behind us in the picture, hands in pockets, stand three congenitally red-eyed intruders in my documentary.

To an unfamiliar reader, this is how John the Baptist comes across in the Gospels: a character whose brief cameo has no seeming connection to the storyline. But as we'll see, John was anything but peripheral to the messianic drama; he is rather the preface to it.

The biblical prophet Malachi (which my spell check is convinced should be *mariachi;* while that would be festive, it's just not the case) declared to Israel four hundred years before the birth of Christ that the next big thing in God's unfolding plan of salvation was not the coming of the Messiah but the coming of his herald: a great prophet who would announce the coming king.

> I will send my messenger, who will prepare the way before me. Then suddenly the Lord you are seeking will come. (Malachi 3:1)

> See, I will send you [one like] the prophet Elijah before that great and dreadful day of the LORD comes. (Malachi 4:5)

The Old Testament describes Elijah as "a man with a garment of hair and with a leather belt around his waist" (2 Kings 1:8), language that the Gospel of Mark uses to describe John the Baptist: "clothing made of camel's hair, with a leather belt around his waist" (Mark 1:6). He came using words reminiscent of Malachi's prophecy: "Prepare the way for the Lord, make straight paths for him" (Mark 1:3). With the appearance of John, the Gospels suggest that the 'one like Elijah' had arrived, and something new was about to happen in Israel.

As best as a timeline can be traced, the ministry of John seems to have lasted about two years, preceding and for just a brief time overlapping the ministry of Jesus. The first-century Jewish historian Josephus provides us with a description of John the Baptist nearly identical to what we know of him from the Gospels.

> John called the baptist . . . was a good man and had urged the Jews to exert themselves to virtue, both as to justice toward one another and reverence towards God.[9]

As is true of most people with ego strength, John seemed immune to social opinion, conventions and status. Subsisting on locusts and honey and living in the wilderness, he camped on the borders of civilization in every possible sense. John's prophetic role was that of a herald, a forerunner whose job was to announce the coming Messiah. John attempted to jar Israel back from a spiritual coma, and to the degree that he succeeded, he provided Jesus with his initial stream of followers. His second role was to bear witness to the Messiah—a sort of celebrity endorsement. And, as Josephus's quote attests, in first-century Israel, John was a spiritual rock star.

John stands as a living, walking—screaming—metaphor. He is the last, and final, in the long line of Old testament prophets, but stands a foot taller then the rest, subsuming in his ministry and message all that the former prophets had said, warned and predicted. In John's pointing to Jesus it's as if the entire Old Testament were pointing to him, saying, "This is the guy we're talking about!"

The downside of not being a respecter of persons, is, well, not being a respecter of persons. Sometime after naming Jesus as the Messiah, John made public accusations concerning King Herod's adulterous relationship with his sister-in-law. Herod, valuing freedom of expression about as much as any tyrant might, had him imprisoned and executed.

Herod probably thought that with John's death his troubles were over, not realizing that John was simply the warm-up band. Having fulfilled all of the major Old Testament birth prophecies of the Messiah, and having received a glowing endorsement and an initial stream of followers from Israel's reigning prophet, Jesus was only getting started. With John gone, all eyes in Israel will now turn solely to him.

2 VULGAR

Coarse Words, Shocking Speech

At roughly the age of thirty, the time when most young men are just moving out of their parents' basement, Jesus began his life's work. His time in the public eye lasted roughly three years, but that still translates into hundreds of spoken messages. Itinerant preaching is similar to political canvassing (except the messages are generally true, not generally lies) in that the speaker often uses a basic palette of messages, slightly altered as the occasion or audience requires. We can therefore presume that Jesus gave versions of the same message on multiple occasions and that preserved within the Gospels are what Jesus' followers considered his essential, stock teachings.

We should also presume that Jesus' spoken sermons and messages were not nearly so compact as they are found in the Bible. If, as the Gospels imply, Jesus preached for many hours, we're missing a good bit of discourse and—who knows?—maybe even some first-century humor, whatever that might have looked like. But this sort of abbreviation is common to all reporting. When a newspaper headline reads "President okays labor agreement,"[1] we don't assume that the president sat stupefied for a three-hour meeting, only to rise at the end of it and decree, "Okay." Most of Jesus' sayings have a poetic phrasing and rhythm to them because they were meant to be delivered verbally and memorized.

"The first shall be last and the last shall be first," for example, is a tightly packed conceptual suitcase made to travel well to another audience or culture, even down through the ages.

In first-century Judaism rabbis employed disciples to memorize, preserve and pass on their key sayings. Disciples were not groupies or some amp-toting road crew but more in the order of apprentices. Jesus chose twelve such disciples:

> Simon (whom he named Peter), his brother Andrew, James, John, Philip, Bartholomew, Matthew, Thomas, James son of Alphaeus, Simon who was called the Zealot, Judas son of James, and Judas Iscariot, who became a traitor. (Luke 6:14-16)

Jesus' selection of twelve, as opposed to fourteen or four, was clearly a symbolic act. Israel as a nation was a composite of twelve separate tribes, so the choosing of twelve disciples communicated a message to the effect of "Here is the true Israel" or "I'm putting the old Israel up for auction on eBay" or something. Understandably, this less than subtle message would not have been warmly received by Israel's leaders.

For the three years that followed, these twelve men would eat, sleep and absorb everything Jesus did and said. And as we turn to their record of his teachings within the Gospels, we find summarizing an easier task than we might have imagined, for by and large Jesus' sermons fit snugly under the heading "The Kingdom of God."

> Jesus traveled about from one town and village to another, proclaiming the good news of the kingdom of God. The Twelve were with him. (Luke 8:1)

Or to flip it around, to understand the nature of the kingdom of God—its values, how one enters it and who reigns over it—is to have understood the teaching of Jesus.

Kingdom Come

> [Jesus] went to Nazareth, where he had been brought up, and on the Sabbath day he went into the synagogue, as was his custom. And he stood up to read. The scroll of the prophet Isaiah was handed to him. Unrolling it, he found the place where it is written:
>
> > "The Spirit of the Lord is on me,
> >> because he has anointed me
> >> to preach good news to the poor.
> > He has sent me to proclaim freedom for the prisoners
> >> and recovery of sight for the blind,
> > to release the oppressed,
> >> to proclaim the year of the Lord's favor."
>
> Then he rolled up the scroll, gave it back to the attendant and sat down. The eyes of everyone in the synagogue were fastened on him, and he began by saying to them, "Today this scripture is fulfilled in your hearing." (Luke 4:16-21)

As Jesus walked from town to town, it was not unusual for an inquisitive soul to approach with a question and receive a response from him as comprehensible as Beowulf. But here, in the opening words of his public ministry, Jesus was anything but veiled: "The Messiah has come, and by the way, you're looking at him." The prophecy he read, from the book of Isaiah, is a clear reference to the coming of the Messiah, and in saying it had been fulfilled, Jesus placed the Messiah's crown upon his own head, to the shock of all in attendance.

Sometimes, when sitting in a formal or solemn gathering such as a church service, I picture what would happen if I stood up and blurted out a string of obscenities. From there, I imagine other humiliating scenarios: chuckling during a funeral, oinking like a pig during the exchange of vows at a wedding—basically, the most socially inappropriate behavior conceivable. I'm really not sure why I do this—maybe I lacked adequate human contact at an early age or was left behind on a family trip to the circus, who knows—but imagining the utter humiliation such behavior would cause me, especially in the midst of close friends and family, gives me considerable empathy for Jesus in this story.

The scene took place in Nazareth, where Jesus was raised, and the synagogue would have been packed with friends, family, peers, just about everyone who knew him from childhood. And in front of them all he stood and made this shocking confession, knowing that most, if not all, would think he had lost his mind. Even for the Messiah, this had to take some serious testosterone. Due to my own inflated sense of dignity, I'm ashamed to admit that I would have rather oinked like a pig in front of loved ones than make such an outrageous statement.

But with Jesus, profundity lurked not only in what he said but also in what he left unsaid, when he was absent as much as when he was present. Jesus' public reading in the synagogue came from what we now call chapter 61 in the book of Isaiah. If you look up the verse in its context, you'll notice that he stopped short of its completion:

. . . to proclaim the year of the LORD's favor
and the day of vengeance of our God (Isaiah 61:2)

Jesus said that he had come "to proclaim the year of the Lord's favor," but the text continues on to state, "and the day of vengeance of our God" (Isaiah 61:2). Why didn't Jesus read the entire sentence?

Jesus' censorship highlights the nature of his ministry. The second part of the verse—the Day of Judgment—will come soon enough, but that day is not today. Jesus was proclaiming grace, forgiveness, the year of the Lord's favor: "Come in now and all debts will be canceled." This general description, more than any specific act, reveals the true heart of

Jesus' ministry, because it is as he himself defined it.

Bono, famed humanitarian, musician and iPod user, gave this insightful summary of Jesus' category-shattering ministry of grace.

> At the center of all religions is the idea of Karma. You know, what you put out comes back to you: an eye for an eye, a tooth for a tooth, or in physics—in physical laws—every action is met by an equal or an opposite one. It's clear to me that Karma is at the very heart of the universe. I'm absolutely sure of it. And yet, along comes this idea called Grace to upend all that "as you reap, so you will sow" stuff. Grace defies reason and logic. Love interrupts, if you like, the consequences of your actions, which in my case is very good news indeed, because I've done a lot of stupid stuff. . . .
>
> The point of the death of Christ is that Christ took on the sins of the world, so that what we put out did not come back to us, and that our sinful nature does not reap the obvious death. That's the point. It should keep us humbled. . . . It's not our own good works that get us through the gates of heaven.[2]

Whatever else the kingdom of God may be, it is about grace. Under this new administration, unimaginable terms of surrender are offered to all moral and spiritual rebels. "Turn yourselves in and all crimes will be forgotten, all records expunged. Throw down your guns!" Having delivered these inaugural words in the synagogue at Nazareth, the ministry of Jesus starts with a gunshot, summoning the attention of all Israel and beginning a race that would last roughly three years, until it ended in a state-sanctioned lynching.

A Kingdom of Losers

> Large crowds from Galilee, the Decapolis, Jerusalem, Judea and the region across the Jordan followed [Jesus].

Now when he saw the crowds, he went up on a mountainside and sat down. His disciples came to him, and he began to teach them, saying:

"Blessed are the poor in spirit,
   for theirs is the kingdom of heaven.
Blessed are those who mourn,
   for they will be comforted.
Blessed are the meek,
   for they will inherit the earth.
Blessed are those who hunger and thirst for righteousness,
   for they will be filled.
Blessed are the merciful,
   for they will be shown mercy.
Blessed are the pure in heart,
   for they will see God.
Blessed are the peacemakers,
   for they will be called sons of God.
Blessed are those who are persecuted because of
     righteousness,
   for theirs is the kingdom of heaven.

"Blessed are you when people insult you, persecute you and falsely say all kinds of evil against you because of me. Rejoice and be glad, because great is your reward in heaven, for in the same way they persecuted the prophets who were before you." (Matthew 4:25—5:12)

Jesus' Sermon on the Mount generally, and these "beatitudes" specifically, are a little like an Italian opera: everyone agrees that the words are beautiful, we just have no idea what he's saying.

What, for example, could he possibly have meant by such obvious contradictions as "blessed ["happy," or "lucky"] are the poor in spirit ["unhappy," or "unlucky"]"? There seem to be two answers, both related to the admittance policy of the kingdom of God.

"Everyone is welcome." This is Article 1 of the kingdom's admission policy. Fidel Castro, enraged by all the people escaping his Communist government in Cuba to take refuge in the United States, emptied his prisons and put them all on boats bound for Miami Beach. Did we send them back? No. On principle, everyone is welcome in the United States: give us your tired, your poor, your huddled masses, and all that stuff.

"Did I say 'everyone'? Well, not really everyone." This is Article 2 of the admission policy. What Jesus was describing in the Beatitudes is the state of heart of a person who is best able to receive the message of the kingdom. And that clearly is not everybody. The entrance restriction lies not with the kingdom itself—all really are welcome—but with the heart of the person who rejects it.

To better understand this point, we'll need momentary use of a trite metaphor; let's go with a fireplace. Some hearts are like a fireplace stuffed with dry kindling and a Duraflame log: the slightest spark, and it will all go up like a Roman candle. Other hearts, however—mushy, moldy, magotty—wouldn't light if they were doused with propane and wired to C-4 explosives. As a result, when people come in contact with the message of the kingdom, they react differently. Some immediately spark to it. Others take time to warm to it. Still others have slipped below the freezing point—tragically, there seems to be nothing within them for the message to ignite.

The reason why being poor in spirit, mourning, being lowly and thirsting for righteousness are blessed states is that they permit no delusions that life and happiness can be found in sex, wealth, drugs, status, travel, entertainment or anything that has a remote control. A desperate alcoholic and a repentant prostitute in such an economy are closer to finding

God because they experience a real hunger for God—the awareness that only God can meet their hunger. The religiously numb, wealthy, self-sufficient and morally jaded are oblivious to the true state of their own heart, mistakenly thinking that they are already in the kingdom, that there is no kingdom or that being in the kingdom is of no consequence. Such self-delusion is the opposite of being "blessed." Jesus distills the essence of our lives down to a simple question: What do you crave? Some hunger and thirst for the kingdom; some hunger and thirst for everything but. Some enter the kingdom; some do not.

Martin Luther, the German leader of the Protestant Reformation, was asked when exactly he entered God's kingdom and came to faith. His response was *"in cloaca,"* which sounds spiritual until you translate it to English: it means "on the toilet." Now, Luther was unquestionably a man with "issues," so it's quite possible that this *was* the actual location. But many scholars believe that he was using a metaphor, popular in the Middle Ages, for "humility" and "humbling oneself." And if you think about it, it's a darn good metaphor for humility, for if there is ever a time or place where you are completely humble, it is here. There is no pretense, no facade, no pride, no image management—you are what you are. The toilet is ground zero for humanity. The key to the kingdom is in fact the key to the rest room.

Here, as with all of Jesus' lessons, we need to proceed carefully. The main point of his teaching was to shock the heart, stimulate a pulse and impart life. The picture Jesus paints of the kingdom of God is not some Disneyworld experience where everyone but Adolf Hitler gets a day pass. It's a description meant to jolt and shock, which might not be a bad idea for us—what *do* we hunger and thirst for?

Conduct in the Kingdom

The teachers of the law and the Pharisees brought in a woman caught in adultery. They made her stand before the group and said to Jesus, "Teacher, this woman was caught in the act of adultery. In the Law Moses commanded us to stone such women. Now what do you say?" They were using this question as a trap, in order to have a basis for accusing him.

But Jesus bent down and started to write on the ground with his finger. When they kept on questioning him, he straightened up and said to them, "If any one of you is without sin, let him be the first to throw a stone at her." Again he stooped down and wrote on the ground.

At this, those who heard began to go away one at a time, the older ones first, until only Jesus was left, with the woman still standing there. Jesus straightened up and asked her, "Woman, where are they? Has no one condemned you?"

"No one, sir," she said.

"Then neither do I condemn you," Jesus declared. "Go now and leave your life of sin." (John 8:3-11)

In his book *Les Misérables* (it's like the play, only the characters don't sing), Victor Hugo sets up a conflict between his two main characters, Inspector Javert and Jean Valjean, representing the tension between justice and mercy, law and grace. Jean Valjean is an escaped parolee who is given grace, mercy and a small fortune by a kindly bishop; Javert is the legalistic police inspector who can find no rest until he brings Valjean to justice.

This same tension stretches between Jesus and the religious legalists of his day. The Pharisees loved the Law of Moses and arrived at a formula for righteousness yielded by the sum of 248 commandments, 365 prohibitions and more than 1,500 hedge laws (peripheral laws created to keep from even approaching a breach of the real laws). In an administration

where justice and observance of the law are the only values, mercy becomes the greatest evil, and transgressors become hunted fugitives. And
so the Pharisees set a trap for Jesus.

The trap, as far as sinister and nefarious plots go, was ingenius.
Roman-occupied Israel could not exercise capital punishment, so if
Jesus said, "Stone her," as the Law of Moses demanded for this offense,
he was likely to be seized by the Roman militia. If, on the other hand, he
said, "Let her go," then he was guilty of undermining the Mosaic Law,
an action that could be used to turn Israel against him. As I said, quite
ingenius. The unfortunate woman in this passage was nothing more
than bait. Her life, her shame: inconsequential.

Jesus, clearly no stranger to martial arts, used his attackers' forward
momentum against them, flipping the situation and placing *them* in an
ethical dilemma: "If I throw the stone, I'll be saying I'm sinless, which
could turn the people against me!" The religious leaders, having been
caught in their own trap, dispersed, blank faced and dazed.

Two times during this exchange Jesus stooped to write on the ground
with his finger. Theologians have speculated for a couple millennia
about what Jesus might have been writing, but concentrating on *what*
he wrote misses the point. The important detail is the fact that, as the
experts in the Mosaic law interrogated him, he was writing with his finger, echoing this Old Testament verse: "When the LORD finished speaking to Moses on Mount Sinai, he gave him the two tablets of the Testimony, the tablets of stone inscribed by the finger of God" (Exodus
31:18). The very finger that had written the Law was now writing on the
ground—and being quizzed by the "experts" on the Law's contents.
That's like asking Bill Gates if he knows what a web browser is.

Clearly, Jesus isn't disputing the moral content of the Law—that's not
what this is about. Rather he's challenging a soulless application of it
and a legalistic interpretation that misses the heart behind it. The impact

of Jesus' behavior was perhaps intended more for the woman than for her accusers; she broke the law of God but was forgiven by the Lawgiver. And if the author of the law declares you innocent, then whatever your jury decrees is irrelevant.

The story also provides us with the kingdom's code of conduct: that which is expected of its citizens. The kingdom is about grace, first being its recipient and then, in turn, extending grace to others. "If [someone] sins against you seven times in a day, and seven times comes back to you and says, 'I repent,' forgive him" (Luke 17:4).

But while the economy of grace is about receiving and giving undeserved mercy for wrongs committed, never changing one's habits pillages grace—"Grandma's such a sweet and caring soul—let's empty her bank account." And so Jesus' direction to the woman is "Go now and leave your life of sin." It is called repentance (a change of heart, life, direction), and it is the way kingdom members honor the grace that has been given. They leave behind the habits that led them to the door of grace needing a handout.

Parables: Messengers of the Kingdom

The disciples came to [Jesus] and asked, "Why do you speak to the people in parables?"

He replied, "The knowledge of the secrets of the kingdom of heaven has been given to you, but not to them. Whoever has will be given more, and he will have an abundance. Whoever does not have, even what he has will be taken from him. This is why I speak to them in parables:

'Though seeing, they do not see;
   though hearing, they do not hear or understand.'

In them is fulfilled the prophecy of Isaiah:

'You will be ever hearing but never understanding;
　　you will be ever seeing but never perceiving.
For this people's heart has become calloused;
　　they hardly hear with their ears,
　　and they have closed their eyes.
Otherwise they might see with their eyes,
　　hear with their ears,
understand with their hearts and turn,
　　and I would heal them.'

But blessed are your eyes because they see, and your ears because they hear. For I tell you the truth, many prophets and righteous men longed to see what you see but did not see it, and to hear
what you hear but did not hear it. (Matthew 13:10-17)
　　Jesus spoke all these things to the crowd in parables; he did not
say anything to them without using a parable. (Matthew 13:34)

You really can't appreciate a book or a movie without knowing its
genre. As soon as I know it's a zombie movie, I know to rate the film
based on body count and not acting. Genre is everything. The merit of
the phrase "eggs, chili powder, prune juice and Captain Crunch" can
only be assessed by learning whether the genre is that of a grocery list,
a poem or a recipe. It's a coherent grocery list, a lousy poem and a vile
recipe.
　　To understand a particular section of the Bible, you simply must iden-
tify the genre, for the book as a whole is a quilt of virtually every genre
imaginable. The phrase "God is my rock" (Psalm 18:2) is meant as a
comforting metaphor but would be a rather disturbing statement of
fact—God as igneous sediment. It is a sad reality that a great deal of interpretive error, as well unwarranted criticism of the Bible, stems from a
mislabeling or ignorance of its genres.

The Gospels, thankfully, are pretty straightforward, and so the only question facing readers is asked by the disciples: Why parables? Why did Jesus choose this genre, as opposed to a typical sermon outline? Jesus' answer: the genre *is* the message.

A parable is a lot like a poem, so focusing our mental horsepower on understanding the genre of poetry will help us figure out what Jesus was saying through his use of parables. Let's start our education with a few lines of verse, shall we?

Vital spark of heav'nly flame,
Quit, oh, quit, this mortal frame!
Trembling, hoping, ling'ring, flying,
Oh, the pain, the bliss of dying!
Cease, fond Nature, cease thy strife,
And let me languish into life!

Hark! they whisper; Angels say,
Sister Spirit, come away.
What is this absorbs me quite,
Steals my senses, shuts my sight,
Drowns my spirits, draws my breath?
Tell me, my Soul! can this be Death?

As the poem doesn't make me nauseated, psychotic or depressed, we can safely assume that the author isn't Sylvia Plath. It was written by Alexander Pope. I believe the poem in some way relates to God, which makes sense, for God only knows what Pope could mean by "What is this absorbs me quite." As Pope published the poem, it's safe to assume that he wanted us to understand its meaning; so why, then, didn't he make the meaning clearer?

The point of a poem is to both reveal truth and at the same time obfuscate or conceal it from all who would trample it, skateboard over it or smudge it with oily hands. Like virginity, a poem is garrisoned to the brute, but to the true lover, its petals open. Pope has encrypted his meaning so that only those who have a heart to understand—or "ears to hear," to use Jesus' phrase—will decode its meaning. That's how Pope wanted it. That's why he chose this genre. That's the price of admission.

This is antithetical to the media marketing with which we're daily dosed—sound bites designed to gather the highest possible viewership. Predicated on clarity, frequency, volume, memorability and bandwidth, they're the polar opposite of poems, which seek to whittle down the audience to only an attentive few.

Jesus' response to the disciples' question, and his explanation for speaking in parables, is similar to the rationale behind a poem. The shocking truth is that Jesus doesn't want everyone to understand him. Yes, that's what I said, "Jesus did not want everyone to understand him." To those who don't have a heart to know God, his words will not rhyme (that's a metaphor): they will be meaningless, veiled, trivial, inconsequential or twisted to say something they didn't mean. But to those whose hearts are open (those who have "ears to hear"), they will recognize not only the meaning of the parable but also the identity of the Messiah, who is himself a parable—truth in a disguise, truth veiled. That's how Jesus wants it. That's why he chose this genre. That's the price of admission.

There is great mercy in the literary vehicle of a parable. During an intervention, family and friends confront a loved one who has entered into some kind of destructive behavior with the truth about his or her life. It's a dangerous procedure, only to be performed when a person is in the final sequence of self-destruct and there are many within the blast radius. Yet it's not the procedure itself that's dangerous. When truth is unveiled so openly, so I'm-putting-my-hands-over-my-ears-so-I-can't-hear-you-lalala-lala bluntly, you have eliminated the option of neutrality, of denial, of rationalization. When truth is presented so baldly, all options are narrowed to two, and the hearer must either open their hearts and respond or harden their hearts beyond remedy. An intervention is a last resort.

In cloaking the truth in parables, Jesus allowed for people to be in a process, to be on a spiritual journey, to remain neutral if they chose. The parables are a dog whistle, piercing to the faithful but muted to the masses, graciously allowing the unready to avoid an out-and-out, final confrontation with the truth.

This is what made parables a good genre for the message of the kingdom: a veiled Messiah (the King disguised as a vagrant), a veiled kingdom (a spiritual economy), a veiled message (parables instead of commandments).

The King of the Kingdom

In the beginning was the Word, and the Word was with God, and the Word was God. He was with God in the beginning. . . .

The Word became flesh and made his dwelling among us. (John 1:1-2, 14)

Jesus answered, "I am the way and the truth and the life. No one comes to the Father except through me. If you really knew me, you would know my Father as well. From now on, you do know him and have seen him."

Philip said, "Lord, show us the Father and that will be enough for us."

Jesus answered: "Don't you know me, Philip, even after I have been among you such a long time? Anyone who has seen me has seen the Father. How can you say, 'Show us the Father'? Don't you believe that I am in the Father, and that the Father is in me?" (John 14:6-10)

Kingdom: the concept, and the word itself, is pregnant with the idea of a king. That Jesus viewed himself, and was viewed by his followers, as *that* king is beyond doubt. But, as this is the kingdom of God, who but God could reign over it? Was Jesus claiming to be God?

The Gospels answer that question with an unequivocal "yes"—or "yea, verily," depending on your translation. A casual reading of the Gospels affirms both Jesus' claims to deity—"Anyone who has seen me has seen the Father"—as well as his disciples' apprehension of that fact. The Gospel writers strengthen the case by citing passages from the Old Testament which clearly show the Messiah to be of divine nature, passages like this one from Isaiah:

> To us a child is born . . . And he will be called
>   Wonderful Counselor, Mighty God,
>   Everlasting Father, Prince of Peace. (Isaiah 9:6)

And if Jesus' statements concerning his deity were at times veiled, the message was clearly not lost on his enemies: " 'We are not stoning you for any of these,' replied the Jews, 'but for blasphemy, because you, a mere man, claim to be God' " (John 10:33).

Modern agnosticizing over this claim has sought to rationalize it through the notion that Jesus may have believed in the divinity of all persons. This idea rests on what is most loathed about movies like *Titanic* or *The Kingdom of Heaven:* characters are equipped with modern-day sensibilities and worldviews, and plopped into a revisionist past, immune to the prejudices, values and beliefs of the world the director has made them occupy.

The idea that we are all part of God, and that divinity resides within each of us, is simply not a possible meaning for Jesus' words and actions. Jesus was a *Jew;* the disciples were *Jews;* they lived in *Israel.* They were not raised watching *Star Wars* and thinking of God as a "Force" or electrical current, but on the Old Testament, which worshiped a personal God as far above humans as we are above mollusks. To presume that Jesus believed in the divinity of all is to be guilty of our own revisionist history, cramming an enlightened guru Jesus into a time capsule and transporting him back from the New Age and into first-century Israel. To presume this is also to think that the idea of each of us housing a fragment of the parceled-out Almighty is more intellectually sound or takes less faith than trusting in Jesus' self-awareness as the one and only deity. It isn't and it doesn't.

Still others have sought to make peace with Jesus' claim to be God by proposing that it was attributed to him later or developed as a belief over time. But the apostle Paul's letters to the Galatians, Thessalonians, Philippians and Corinthians can be solidly placed between A.D. 50 and 60, just a couple decades after the death of Christ (around A.D. 30–33), and in those letters we find both Paul's affirmation that Jesus was "in very nature God" (Philippians 2:6) and that what he taught, all the churches believed (Galatians 1:22, 23). In fact, embedded within these letters are creeds that are even older, dating back to just a few years after the death of Jesus, and which affirm the early, and universal, Christian belief in Christ's deity. Take a look at one of the early embedded creeds within Paul's letter to the Colossians:

He is the image of the invisible God, the firstborn over all creation. For by him all things were created: things in heaven and on earth, visible and invisible, whether thrones or powers or rulers or authorities; all things were created by him and for him. He is before all things, and in him all things hold together. And he is the head of the body, the church; he is the beginning and the firstborn from among the dead, so that in everything he might have the supremacy. For God was pleased to have all his fullness dwell in him. (Colossians 1:15-19)

In *The World's Great Religions,* Huston Smith observes, "Only two people ever astounded their contemporaries so much that the question they evoked was not 'Who is he?' but *'What is he?'* They were Jesus and Buddha. The answers these two gave were exactly the opposite. Buddha said unequivocally that he was a mere man, not a god—almost as if he foresaw later attempts to worship him. Jesus, on the other hand, claimed . . . to be divine."[3]

Every now and then something chomps its way up the food chain that is difficult for humans to classify. It's bizarre, for example, that a whale is classified as a mammal. As I do not possess a spout hole, it's hard for me to see how we share a connection. At the same time, I can see that a whale isn't exactly a fish either.

For a religious or moral teacher to claim to be God moves him out of the nice, safe, perhaps even patronizing phylum of religious leader, and it forces us to place him within one of three families: the family of liars (religious leaders who lied about who and what they were), the family of lunatics (religious leaders who actually believed they were God but were not), or the family of God (in this case, the Son of).

In the world of religious leaders, Jesus is often lumped in with other great religious leaders, including Moses, Muhammad and Buddha. But frankly, he doesn't fit. On the surface he looks like a wonderful religious leader who helped shape the world of faith and morals, but his claim to be God makes him a different species altogether.

This is the last, and clearly most challenging, of Jesus' kingdom teachings: the nature and identity of the King. It is challenging because it puts us in an uncomfortable dilemma, described well by the famed Oxford professor C. S. Lewis:

A man who was merely a man and said the sort of things Jesus said would not be a great moral teacher. He would either be a lunatic—on a level with the man who says he is a poached egg—or else he would be the Devil of Hell. You must make your choice. Either this man was, and is, the Son of God: or else a mad man or something worse. [4]

Aware that such audacious claims would invite skepticism, Jesus asked questions like "Which is easier: to say to the paralytic, 'Your sins are forgiven,' or to say, 'Get up, take your mat and walk'?" (Mark 2:9). Try it yourself: is it easier to make an outrageous claim than to perform an outrageous miracle? "I am the world's rightful pope." "I command you, 2004 Ford Windstar, to rise from the driveway."

I found making the outrageous claim significantly easier, and that, I take it, was Jesus' point as he proceeded to heal a paralytic and defend his claim to forgive sin. " 'But that you may know that the Son of Man has authority on earth to forgive sins.' . . . He said to the paralytic, 'I tell you, get up, take your mat and go home' " (Mark 2:10, 11).

Jesus was aware that the power and authority that he claimed to possess would need to be demonstrated. As we turn to the miracles of Jesus we'll see what he did about that.

3   MARVEL
Super Power

No matter how great the stereo, music coming out of only one speaker will sound like it's being played on the intercom at Foodworld, which is why speakers—and ears, for that matter—are available in pairs. In the ministry of Jesus, his teachings and miracles were essentially two different speakers playing the same song, his miracles complementing and authenticating his teaching. And that's why the miracles of Jesus always had a point: Jesus was running a ministry, not a sideshow.

Here is the first recorded miracle of Jesus' ministry, the famed turning of water into wine.

> Nearby stood six stone water jars, the kind used by the Jews for ceremonial washing, each holding from twenty to thirty gallons.
>
> Jesus said to the servants, "Fill the jars with water"; so they filled them to the brim.
>
> Then he told them, "Now draw some out and take it to the master of the banquet."
>
> They did so, and the master of the banquet tasted the water that had been turned into wine. (John 2:6-9)

Armed with the assumption that there is always a point, look for details in the picture that might hint at the message. See those massive stone water jars there? They kind of remind me of those Ten Commandment-engraved monoliths that Moses hauled down from the top of

Mount Sinai. Well, that could be a stretch, but regardless, the water inside the stone jars was used for "ceremonial washing"—a procedure prescribed in the Law of Moses that symbolically cleansed of moral impurity. So you have this stone-water-Law-of-Moses-ceremonial-cleansing-Old Covenant theme going on. Add to that the imagery of a wedding, including the bridegroom coming for his bride. So, as Jesus took the stone jars and turned the clear water inside into crimson wine, he was leaving behind a Post-It note saying something like "The Messiah (the bridegroom) has come for the bride (Israel), and my mission is to bring new life and meaning to the old commandments, establish a new covenant and cleanse sin—not symbolically by water but in reality through my blood." Nuances of interpretation may vary, but you see the point—not the point of this miracle but the point about miracles having a point, which was my point.

The Gospels typically place Jesus' miracles in direct relation to the teaching content before or after it. That Jesus' miracles and message went hand in hand is without doubt; whether their correspondence was always so rigidly observed is harder to say. The fact is, they were anything but random in nature and usually fell into one of the following categories:

- The miracle is an object lesson for the disciples.
- The miracle points to Jesus' identity as the Messiah by demonstrating his power over sin, sickness or Satan.
- The miracle exemplifies the importance of faith.
- The miracle in some way is evidence of divinity, manifesting power that is the prerogative of God alone.

While even the most skeptical of readers accept the basic historical reliability of Jesus' teachings, his miracles require faith. But it should be acknowledged at the outset that Jesus' miracles come with some pretty weighty historical evidence, namely the testimony of his enemies.

> They brought him a demon-possessed man who was blind and
> mute, and Jesus healed him, so that he could both talk and see.
> All the people were astonished and said, "Could this be the Son of
> David?"
> But when the Pharisees heard this, they said, "It is only by Bee-
> lzebub, the prince of demons, that this fellow drives out demons."
> (Matthew 12:22-24)

Even Jesus' opponents did not deny his miracles, leaving them to
ratchet down their attack to an argument about the source of his power
(only one rung up in the hierarchy of argumentation from "Oh yeah? Sez
who?"). It should also be remembered that this was not a naive audience; magicians, scam artists and peddlers of snake oil were as recognizable to the Jews back then as they are to us today. No, if discrediting
Jesus' miracles or casting doubt on them was viable, it certainly would
have been used against him, so we must assume that people known to
be blind, saw, and those who couldn't walk, walked, and Jesus' enemies
had to search elsewhere for ammunition to use against him. With that as
our introduction, we'll double-click on each of the major categories of
Jesus' miracles.

The Power of Faith

> [In Capernaum] a centurion's servant, whom his master valued
> highly, was sick and about to die. The centurion heard of Jesus
> and sent some elders of the Jews to him, asking him to come and
> heal his servant. When they came to Jesus, they pleaded earnestly
> with him, "This man deserves to have you do this, because he
> loves our nation and has built our synagogue." So Jesus went with
> them.

He was not far from the house when the centurion sent friends to say to him: "Lord, don't trouble yourself, for I do not deserve to have you come under my roof. That is why I did not even consider myself worthy to come to you. But say the word, and my servant will be healed. For I myself am a man under authority, with soldiers under me. I tell this one, 'Go,' and he goes; and that one, 'Come,' and he comes. I say to my servant, 'Do this,' and he does it."

When Jesus heard this, he was amazed at him, and turning to the crowd following him, he said, "I tell you, I have not found such great faith even in Israel." (Luke 7:2-9)

Jesus said to them, "Only in his hometown, among his relatives and in his own house is a prophet without honor." He could not do any miracles there, except lay his hands on a few sick people and heal them. And he was amazed at their lack of faith. (Mark 6:4-6)

Jesus' miracles were seldom performed independent of a teaching message. But as these two stories demonstrate, they were seldom performed independent of faith either. The three-plus years of Jesus' public ministry were amazing days, so in the Gospels the word *amazed* is about as worn as the word *dude* is today. Yet the Gospels record only two times when Jesus himself was amazed, and both are emotional reactions to faith: Jesus stood amazed at the faith possessed by a Roman centurion and the apparent lack of it within the nation of Israel (Luke 7:9).

In speaking about miracles, I don't mean the "miracle" of childbirth or laughter or hope or antibodies or penicillin. I mean the type of miracle in which one minute there's no one sitting next to you on the bus and the next there's a penguin playing the mandolin—I mean things that don't typically happen (no disrespect to the miracles that occur in the natural order of things).

There are, in fact, reports of modern-day miracles. You won't read about them at the newstand, though the *Enquirer* may cover the occasional sighting of Elvis over Tokyo or the birth of a human-goat child. But the reports are there if you know where to look.

The *JESUS* film project has taken the Gospel of Luke and put it on film. Having seen the film, I'm doubtful that it will be remembered for its cinematography. Or its acting. Or its special effects. Or its art direction. Or . . . Yet it's been translated into thousands of languages and dialects and shown around the world. At last count, almost two-thirds of the planet had viewed the film—more than 5.7 billion people, just eeking out *Zoolander* by 5.6 billion for the "most viewed film of all time." In their annual reports, leaders of the *JESUS* film ministry relate with mild matter-of-factness stories of the blind seeing, the deaf hearing and hundreds of other miracles. Consider, for example, this account from Indonesia that I pulled out of their archives.

Mrs. Peni of Purwonegoro, Indonesia, had been blind for four years. But someone told her about the *JESUS* film, where Jesus heals a blind man. She asked her youngest daughter to guide her to the film showing so she could hear the story even if she couldn't see the picture.

When the scene was shown where the blind man asks Jesus to heal him. Mrs. Peni shouted out, "I want to see too!" A few moments later, as the film showed Jesus being nailed to the cross, her vision was restored.

At a town meeting some time later, the Muslim officials wanted to ridicule her and prove that she really had not been healed. They asked her to come to the front and light a candle. Mrs. Peni got up from her seat and confidently strode to the front. Then, as everyone watched, she picked up the matches and lit the candle. Forty

Muslims decided to trust Christ after seeing this.

The film team was brought back to her village because everyone wanted to see the film about the man who healed Mrs. Peni. Thirty-five hundred people attended the showing and a new church was started in the village.[1]

Admittedly, it's not as enthralling as the birth of a human-goat baby, but still, it's pretty amazing. Now, perhaps there are alternative explanations to this being a miracle. Perhaps if she had been watching *Aliens* and had cried out to have four or five eyes and a retractable jaw full of carnivore teeth, she would have begun to grow them. Perhaps. But proving or disproving this story's veracity is not my point.

Here is the point: Some years ago I interviewed a member of the organization's leadership and remarked that their ministry used to publish these miraculous accounts but no longer did so, and I was curious as to why. The answer was as simple as it was disturbing: "We don't share those stories as much in the U.S., because where there is no faith, miracles actually produce skepticism. It does the exact opposite of what it was intended to do: encourage belief."

At a certain point, Jesus didn't feel compelled to feed people's insatiable appetite for the sensational. If that alone is what drew them, then sooner or later they would find other shiny objects to alleviate their boredom and stop coming to the show. His miracles were meant to encourage faith, not serve as a substitute for it. Those who humbly came to Jesus always found their faith rewarded. But those who remained passive or indifferent, demanding a sign or miracle, would find themselves waiting and waiting and waiting.

I think it's normal to seek evidence, proof and answers—to be in process in one's spiritual journey. But as G. K. Chesterton observed: "the purpose of an open mind is the same as that of an *open* mouth, that it might close on something!" The point of a journey is to arrive at a destination, and I suspect that those who always need more proof and are never satisfied with the answers they're given are not really looking to arrive anyplace.

Power in the Dark

When Jesus stepped ashore, he was met by a demon-possessed man from the town. For a long time this man had not worn clothes or lived in a house, but had lived in the tombs. When he saw Jesus, he cried out and fell at his feet, shouting at the top of his voice, "What do you want with me, Jesus, Son of the Most High God? I beg you, don't torture me!" For Jesus had commanded the evil spirit to come out of the man. Many times it had seized him, and though he was chained hand and foot and kept under guard, he had broken his chains and had been driven by the demon into solitary places.

Jesus asked him, "What is your name?"

"Legion," he replied, because many demons had gone into him. And they begged him repeatedly not to order them to go into the Abyss.

A large herd of pigs was feeding there on the hillside. The demons begged Jesus to let them go into them, and he gave them permission. When the demons came out of the man, they went into the pigs, and the herd rushed down the steep bank into the lake and was drowned.

When those tending the pigs saw what had happened, they ran off and reported this in the town and countryside, and the people went out to see what had happened. When they came to Jesus, they found the man from whom the demons had gone out, sitting at Jesus' feet, dressed and in his right mind; and they were afraid. (Luke 8:27-35)

Today, about the only place where the devil has credibility is within the music world, where rumors have always sold records. Legend had it that the Rolling Stones met with occult leader Aleister Crowley. Or perhaps that was Anton LaVey, author of the *Satanic Bible.* Groups like AC/DC and Ozzy Osbourne promoted Satanism with an evangelist's zeal, while groups like the Dead Kennedys and the Cramps looked like Satanists but were actually nihilists. And that's where things got really fuzzy. Marketing showed that Satanism sells, so then it was like *Where's Waldo?* with pentagrams hidden on all kinds of album covers. And, I mean, who isn't going to bite the head off a bat if it boosts record sales? But then again Mick Jagger never ages, so either he's smoking formaldehyde or, like, you know, he cut a deal with the devil. And, like I said, there have always been rumors.

The satanic hijinks of rock stars hold little interest for me. But since seeing the film *The Possession of Emily Rose* I've been insanely curious about the phenomenon of possession. I mean, does this stuff really happen, or should we see the story in Luke 8 as perhaps the healing of a man with primitively diagnosed Dissociative Identity Disorder? So I took it upon myself to do some research, my resumé padded with the following credentials: I've seen the *Exorcist* several times; I have a theology degree, and I know the lyrics to "Highway to Hell"—who could be better for the task?

My investigation began with the mother of all possession stories, *The Exorcist.* Fortunately, someone got there before I did, wondering similar questions, and so the research was already completed and contained in Thomas Allen's book *Possessed*, which chronicles the infamous 1949 exorcism. The most fascinating part of Allen's book is the appendix, where he includes the actual diary of the presiding exorcist, the late Father Bowdern. Here are a few, rather creepy excerpts:

March 14: A stool flew across the room and landed with a loud crash, but no one was injured. The mattress of the bed shook, as on many occasions. The shaking continued for two hours.

March 16: Three large bars were observed to be scratched on the boy's stomach. The marks were sharply painful and raised above the skin similar to an engraving. The most distinctive marking was the word "HELL" imprinted on his chest. They would appear as we read through the exorcism.

April 7: During the praying, at least 20 scratches or brands appeared on the boy's body, usually at the mention of "Jesus." The first mark was clearly the number 4; several times four strokes or claw marks of various lengths appeared on his belly and legs. There was considerable profanity and crudeness concerning sexual relations with priests and nuns.[2]

The true-life case behind *The Exorcist* was witnessed, signed and verified by forty-six Jesuit priests, and the child experienced deliverance about the twenty-fifth day after uttering the word "Dominus," which is Latin for "Lord" or "Christ."

While such cases are not common, they are not anomalies either. Apparently each year the Roman Catholic Church records between 800 and 1,300 exorcisms, with Protestant churches reporting figures much higher.[3] Pretty remarkable when you consider that one of the Catholic Church's criteria for an exorcism has been the victim's ability to speak in an ancient language without prior knowledge of it—*yipes*.

It would be inaccurate to say that modern medicine has relegated all such phenomena to the bloodletting, leech-sucking, witch-burning science of the Middle Ages. While Tourette's syndrome, schizophrenia and

Dissociative Identity Disorder have no doubt been wrongly labeled in the superstitious past, there continue to be cases that defy classification. One of the world's most renowned psychiatrists, M. Scott Peck, reports in his book *Glimpses of the Devil* that there is an undeniable—though exceedingly subtle—delineation between psychological disorder and ontological (personal) evil, which he demonstrates through two modern clinical case studies. Peck believes that spiritual evil, in some cases, is the only rational explanation for attending symptoms and metaphysical phenomena, and that, at times, evil manifests itself in patterns that clearly betray intelligence.[4]

The bottom line is that this spiritual confrontation contained in the Gospels should not be dismissed as naive superstition. In fact, the description of Jesus' exorcism contains some resonant signs of authenticity. The story recounts that the man lived in the tombs, wore no clothes, was driven to a solitary place, had abnormal strength, and according to Mark 5:5, "would cry out and cut himself with stones." You find this same recurring behavior in most modern cases: an absorption with death, antisocial behavior, self-destructive actions and some sign of the paranormal. And, not incidentally, in almost every documented case study, such as that of *The Exorcist,* deliverance was secured only through appeal and acquiescence to Jesus Christ.

As demonstrated in the movies, the rite of exorcism has been performed by mere mortals, no doubt in a maelstrom of flailing hands, holy water and Shakespearean English. But the not-to-be-missed emphasis in the story from the Gospel—indeed, the very reason it was recorded—is that Jesus simply said, "Leave," and the demon did. This was not so much a power struggle as a case of the lifeguard saying, "Everybody out of the pool."

We've all heard the raw, reactionary interviews that follow horrific world events. Three common questions inevitably emerge: Why did God allow this to happen? Is God judging us? What sort of evil people would do this? A lot of finger-pointing goes on, and by no means are people without guilt in these evil actions. But from a biblical perspective, a far from innocent party has somehow avoided indictment and slipped out unnoticed.[5] Jesus' demonstration of power over the spiritual forces of darkness was as important in the first century as it is in many parts of the world today where evil, and not government, military, big business or organized crime, is the power to be reckoned with. In fact, in our sophistication maybe *we've* become the ones who are ignorant.

Power of the Kingdom

"A great prophet has appeared among us," they said. "God has come to help his people." This news about Jesus spread throughout Judea and the surrounding country.

John's disciples told him about all these things. Calling two of them, he sent them to the Lord to ask, "Are you the one who was to come, or should we expect someone else?"

When the men came to Jesus, they said, "John the Baptist sent us to you to ask, 'Are you the one who was to come, or should we expect someone else?' "

At that very time Jesus cured many who had diseases, sicknesses and evil spirits, and gave sight to many who were blind. So he replied to the messengers, "Go back and report to John what you have seen and heard: The blind receive sight, the lame walk, those who have leprosy are cured, the deaf hear, the dead are raised, and the good news is preached to the poor." (Luke 7:16-22)

The situation was this: John the Baptist, forerunner of the Messiah, had been thrown into prison. Pacing around his cell, John began to wonder, *Why, if I'm the herald of the Messiah, do I find myself in lockdown instead of occupying the highest office in Jerusalem?* Perhaps he had been mistaken about Jesus being the Messiah. *(Maybe it was another Jesus—Jezuz with a "z"?)* So he sent messengers to Jesus for affirmation, and Jesus' response . . . Well, it will make perfect sense after we take a short detour back to the beginning—the very beginning.

The story of Genesis 1—3, and especially the part about Adam and Eve, was meant to communicate certain fundamental truths about the human condition: why it is as it is and not as it should or could be. Genesis tells us that humankind was a unique creation endowed with the image of the Creator, which was manifested (among other ways) in their free will.

By its very nature, however, free will makes for two unimagined possibilities: a person can freely choose to love you, or they can choose to reject you, even hate you, even murder you. Risks notwithstanding, equipping us with the more powerful free will chip was a choice God freely made.

As the Eden story unfolds, humanity sins, and evil slithers its way into God's creation. The exonerating events of Genesis bear out that evil and corruption were not of God's making but rather the defect— and there is a defect—that resides in human sin and the perverse use of something intrinsically good: free will.

Sin breached the relationship between God and humanity, and when that was severed, like links in a chain, it uncoupled every relationship contingent to it: people with people (wars, murder, racism), man with woman (divorce, broken families), people with nature (alienation, pollution), people with themselves (guilt, shame, fear). Like a broken DNA sequence, the result has been all manner of deformity within creation: Eden now mutated into a mosh pit. Suffering is nothing more nor less than the negative experience of these severed relationships.

Something of the physics of our own experience corroborates the

Genesis account, with so many existential questions constantly merging and crashing into our thoughts with the sense that things ought to be different, that we were made for something better, that our lives should have purpose and meaning, that suffering is an unnatural intrusion, that contentment is an elusive phantom, that certain actions are not simply inconvenient but wrong—evil. I mean, why do we not simply accept life as it is, with all its brokenness? The world is not as it was meant to be, and we all know it. It's fallen and can't get up.

The Old Testament prophets predicted that the coming Messiah would usher in an unprecedented time of peace and restoration of the world: a return to its created state. Familiarity with the Old Testament brings recognition of a common biblical vocabulary employed by the prophets—a repetition of certain metaphors—to describe this messianic age of restoration. Here are two of the more frequent:

> In that day deaf people will hear words read from a book, and the blind will see through the gloom and darkness. . . . When he comes, he will open the eyes of the blind and unplug the ears of the deaf. (Isaiah 29:18; 35:5, NLT)

> Then will the lame leap like a deer,
>   and the mute tongue shout for joy.
> Water will gush forth in the wilderness
>   and streams in the desert. (Isaiah 35:6)

I've watched religious programming where people in the audience are apparently healed. I mean, who really knows, right? But it seems to me that everyone in the audience suffers from the same kinds of maladies: something congenital, something malignant, something internal, something where I have no possible way of knowing if it's truly been fixed. Anyway, given the Old Testament context, it should be clear why Jesus' miracles repeatedly involved giving sight to the blind, hearing to the deaf, and—I want to say "mobility," but it sure sounds dumb—to the lame. It wasn't that the majority of Israel's population in the first century was blind or that working feet were a rare commodity. Jesus was making a point, with deliberate redundancy, to an audience familiar with the Old Testament metaphors, that the messianic kingdom—the kingdom of God—had arrived. Following in its wake, the deaf and blind were able to see and hear, as the lame triumphed over gravity.

And this is the message he gave John's emissaries: the kingdom of God was wherever Jesus walked. "Go back and report to John what you have seen and heard: The blind receive sight, the lame walk, those who have leprosy are cured, the deaf hear, the dead are raised, and the good news is preached to the poor" (Luke 7:22). This was certainly enough for John to interpret the inferred message: "I am the Messiah, and the messianic kingdom has indeed arrived."

Though certainly not an unforeseen development, ultimately, Jesus' rejection by his people postponed the full inauguration of the kingdom. It exists now in the form of a spiritual kingdom, with hearts and lives ruled by the Messiah. But there will come a day when the world will be made right, when the tears of sin, death and disease will be blotted from our eyes. "Then will the lame leap like a deer, and the mute tongue shout for joy" (Isaiah 35:6).

Absolute Power

Jesus made the disciples get into the boat and go on ahead of him to the other side, while he dismissed the crowd. After he had dismissed them, he went up on a mountainside by himself to pray. When evening came, he was there alone, but the boat was already a considerable distance from land, buffeted by the waves because the wind was against it.

During the fourth watch of the night Jesus went out to them, walking on the lake. When the disciples saw him walking on the lake, they were terrified. "It's a ghost," they said, and cried out in fear.

But Jesus immediately said to them: "Take courage! It is I. Don't be afraid."

"Lord, if it's you," Peter replied, "tell me to come to you on the water."

"Come," he said.

Then Peter got down out of the boat, walked on the water and came toward Jesus. But when he saw the wind, he was afraid and, beginning to sink, cried out, "Lord, save me!"

Immediately Jesus reached out his hand and caught him. "You of little faith," he said, "why did you doubt?"

And when they climbed into the boat, the wind died down. Then those who were in the boat worshiped him, saying, "Truly you are the Son of God." (Matthew 14:22-33)

How do you communicate not only that you are the Messiah but that the Messiah is actually God incarnate? This isn't the sort of thing you can easily weave into the conversation—"Instead of asking God to bless the meal, why not ask me instead?" No, this is going to be a pretty delicate subject and one that Jesus would have to demonstrate, allowing people to do their own calculations on a separate piece of paper.

Jesus knew that an unqualified declaration could easily spark a riot, bloodshed, and an abrupt and premature end to his ministry. Israel under Roman occupation was so highly strung that even the introduction of caffeine into the populace could have triggered a revolt or all-out war. The Gospels note Jesus pulling away from the crowds, moving quickly on to other towns or preventing people from speaking about his identity.

At the source of these actions was a serious concern for the flammable fabric that was Israel.

Instead Jesus, with imaginative subtlety, acted out his message. But if his goal was to demonstrate that he was God incarnate, why not fly? Or turn a mountain into meatloaf? Or people into crescent rolls? (I think I'm hungry.) It could be argued that doing any miracle would have made the point about Jesus' divinity, but that's not really true. There are preachers on my cable channels apparently performing miracles, and I just think of them as being crazy—nice people, very nice hairstyles, but crazy. Also, miracles were performed by some of the great prophets of the Old Testament, so Jesus' choice of miracles would need to distinguish him from the more mundane role of prophet.

So, for example, why did Jesus walk on water? The answer is found in the Old Testament book of Job:

He [God] alone stretches out the heavens
and treads on the waves of the sea. (Job 9:8)

To Jews in the first century, this verse was common knowledge— everyone knew that God alone treads the seas. Had the Old Testament said, "God alone veileth himself in the cloak of a Virginia ham" (Virginia ham—*mmm*), then that would have been the miracle. And conversely, if he didn't want people to arrive at this conclusion, this would certainly have been the last thing he would do.

There is also something compelling (and shrewd) in this teaching style. Impressionist painters did something like this in their use of color: they found you could create a vivid green, for example, simply by laying blue and yellow side by side on the canvas, allowing the viewer to mix the color in their mind. Jesus' coupling of miracle with Old Testament Scripture seems to have produced this intended effect.

Throughout the Gospels, Jesus performs many such miracles in order to disclose his unique identity as the Son of God. And he often followed such demonstrations with statements that, when analyzed, were synonymous in content with the miracle, as with this healing of the paralytic:

> Some men brought to him a paralytic, lying on a mat. When Jesus saw their faith, he said to the paralytic, "Take heart, son; your sins are forgiven." (Matthew 9:2)

Isn't that nice? Jesus was forgiving someone of all his sins. A generous offer, considering this man had never sinned against Jesus. In fact, he had never met Jesus. If the blasphemous implications are not obvious to you, try out a similar statement on a random shopper at your local supermarket.

The religious leaders weren't stupid, and it didn't take them long to decrypt the message. "The Pharisees and the teachers of the law began thinking to themselves, 'Who is this fellow who speaks blasphemy? Who can forgive sins but God alone?' " (Luke 5:21). Message received.

Or consider this subliminal advertisement. In the Old Testament book of Zechariah, there is a prophecy concerning a future day when God himself would visit Jerusalem.

> On that day his feet will stand on the Mount of Olives, east of Jerusalem. . . . And on that day there will no longer be traders in the Temple of the LORD. (Zechariah 14:4, 21 NLT)

And so as Jesus approached Jerusalem he stopped purposefully at "Bethany at the Mount of Olives," and then "on reaching Jerusalem, Jesus entered the temple area and began driving out those who were buying and selling [traders] there" (Mark 11:1, 15).

What? You thought he just lost his temper, overturning the tables of the moneychangers? No, he was enacting a message, wisely left unsaid.

A paradox remains just an oxymoron until you 'get it,' and so it is with Jesus, the 'Servant King' and his 'subtle miracles': miracles and messages holding the perfect note of ambiguity. Able to summon those with 'ears to hear' and avoid an all-out confrontation with those who wouldn't.

Impotent Disciples

When Jesus looked up and saw a great crowd coming toward him, he said to Philip, "Where shall we buy bread for these people to eat?" He asked this only to test him, for he already had in mind what he was going to do.

Philip answered him, "Eight months' wages would not buy enough bread for each one to have a bite!"

Another of his disciples, Andrew, Simon Peter's brother, spoke up, "Here is a boy with five small barley loaves and two small fish, but how far will they go among so many?"

Jesus said, "Have the people sit down." There was plenty of grass in that place, and the men sat down, about five thousand of them. Jesus then took the loaves, gave thanks, and distributed to those who were seated as much as they wanted. He did the same with the fish.

When they had all had enough to eat, he said to his disciples, "Gather the pieces that are left over. Let nothing be wasted." So they gathered them and filled twelve baskets with the pieces of the five barley loaves left over by those who had eaten.

After the people saw the miraculous sign that Jesus did, they began to say, "Surely this is the Prophet who is to come into the world." (John 6:5-14)

The phrase "four score and seven years ago" is nonsensical outside the United States (and, I suppose, to those with SAT scores less than

200) because its meaning is culturally bound.[6] Likewise, certain actions and phrases within the Gospels had the cultural resonance of the Gettysburg Address to their Jewish audience, but they're all but lost on us.

The crowds had walked hours to hear Jesus speak. It was now getting late, and being slightly east of nowhere, the people had no place to find a meal. Jesus asked his disciples how they were planning to address this brewing problem of five thousand hearty, agrarian appetites desperately in need of food. The disciples intelligently began to panic as they thought through the relatively few available options (pizza delivery was still two thousand years in the future). One disciple, Andrew, industriously rounded up several loaves and fish from a child's lunch but then asked forlornly, "How far will they go among so many?" Not very far, Andrew, not very far.

Once the disciples' energy and ingenuity were spent, Jesus took the portion they had mustered and turned it into a banquet large enough to feed an army—or five thousand peasants, as the case may be.

To the crowd, the miraculous appearing of bread enough to feed the masses—in the middle of nowhere—would have immediately brought to mind God's miraculous provision of manna in the wilderness for the starving Israelites (Exodus 16), underscoring Jesus' messianic identity (as well as his deity). But for the disciples, there was a different message altogether. When people were done eating, Jesus instructed his disciples to pick up the remaining scraps, and they gathered twelve basketfuls of leftovers.

Hold on! Twelve—where have we heard that number before? It's how many doughnuts are in a dozen? True, but I was thinking of the fact that there were twelve disciples and twelve baskets of food. This couldn't have been coincidence, so let's try to piece this together.

Once Jesus was gone, his disciples would be left to carry on the ministry. They would be responsible for meeting the spiritual hunger of the masses, and yet, in and of themselves, they were inadequate for the task. Spiritually speaking, they represented the equivalent of a few loaves and a smelly fish.

Why the need for the lesson? Perhaps the disciples had become artificially buoyed by being in Jesus' inner circle and had lost sight of their inadequacy. Or more likely they were simply unaware of what Jesus knew only too well: his time with them was running out. But when Jesus put them on the spot, they became painfully aware of their lack. As public humiliation often does, this provided a teachable moment. Jesus stepped in and demonstrated, by way of a miracle, that through God's empowerment and provision they would have all they needed to accomplish their task—provided, that is, that God was always catering the affair. And later, as they gathered twelve basketfuls of leftovers, they would no doubt be sobered to the awesome responsibility and honor they bore as God's chosen vessels to feed his people.

And so the miracle of feeding the five thousand is not a lesson about how to share what's in our lunchbox. Among other things, it was an object lesson for the disciples. I might have lost a few people with that example, so here's a quicker and easier one.

They came to Bethsaida, and some people brought a blind man and begged Jesus to touch him. He took the blind man by the hand and led him outside the village. When he had spit on the man's eyes and put his hands on him, Jesus asked, "Do you see anything?"

He looked up and said, "I see people; they look like trees walking around."

Once more Jesus put his hands on the man's eyes. Then his eyes were opened, his sight was restored, and he saw everything clearly. (Mark 8:22-25)

I have no doubts about the potency of Jesus' saliva; I'm willing to bet that Jesus could have healed this guy's sight on the first shot if he had wanted to. But instead, the man's eyesight was only partially restored, his vision still blurred, able to make out contours but not details. Kind of sounds like the disciples doesn't it? Just listen to their discussion with Jesus immediately prior to this healing of the blind man:

"Be careful," Jesus warned [the disciples]. "Watch out for the yeast of the Pharisees and that of Herod."

They discussed this with one another and said, "It is because we have no bread."

Aware of their discussion, Jesus asked them: "Why are you talking about having no bread? Do you still not see or understand? Are your hearts hardened?" (Mark 8:15-17)

"Watch out for the yeast of the Pharisees," says Jesus.

"I think Jesus is angry that we didn't buy any bread," say the disciples.

The healing of the blind man was meant to parallel the disciples' partial comprehension of Jesus and his mission. They saw, but they didn't see, not fully. They understood the broader contours but were confused by much of what Jesus did and said. This was another miracle as object lesson.

Throughout the Gospels, you'll find many of these after-school lessons for a class of disciples in need of special tutoring for final exams were drawing closer, when they would be left to carry on the ministry without their teacher.

Before leaving the subject of miracles, I want to mention a last and final layer of meaning contained within the miracles of Jesus. In the Gospels, physical disease, disability and death carry symbolic or metaphoric reference to the deeper reality of spiritual malignancy and souls terminally ill from the effects of sin. For example, many people to whom Jesus spoke were spiritually blind: blind to their own sin, blind to their need for repentance, as well as blind to the identity of Jesus. Jesus' interaction with those who were physically blind certainly has this as a backdrop of meaning. Leprosy, another common disease in the Gospels, eats away at the skin all the while numbing the body's ability to perceive the damage (lepers lose the sensation of pain). If there were a better metaphor for the concurrent soul-ravaging and conscience-numbing effects of sin, I'd love to hear it.

First century Judaism took the connection between the spiritual and physical so concretely that those with such diseases were automatically labeled as "sinners." Thus to heal someone of blindness or leprosy intrinsically carried the meaning of spiritual forgiveness and moral cleansing. With that in mind we'll close this section with the haunting question that Jesus asked a man who had been an invalid for thirty-eight years.

When Jesus saw him lying there and learned that he had been in this condition for a long time, he asked him, "Do you want to get well?" (John 5:6)

"Do you want to get well?" I should think the answer would be rather obvious, but seen through a spiritual lens, as this man perhaps would have, it's anything but rhetorical. I mean, if you could be healed of lust or greed or anger or pride or lying, would you really want to? Just like this crippled man whose identity was defined by his disability, our lives too are arranged around such moral furniture and would look quite different without them. And what if "getting well" spiritually meant a painful amputation of a beloved habit, the denial of a personal passion or the death of a dream? Would you still want to be well? When the patient is our souls and not our bodies, everything changes. The issue is no longer "Can Jesus heal?" but "Do I want to get well?" And that's perhaps the better, more gospelesque, question to take with us from Jesus' miracles.

4   SCANDALON

The Final Offense

The Gospels of Matthew, Mark and Luke all contain a hinge story that takes the body of Jesus' ministry and breaks it in two. Leading up to this point, Jesus demonstrated his identity in every way imaginable, but this particular interaction was the turning point when his disciples fully recognized their companion—or rather, their companion allowed himself to be recognized.

> Jesus and his disciples went on to the villages around Caesarea Philippi. On the way he asked them, "Who do people say I am?"
>
> They replied, "Some say John the Baptist; others say Elijah; and still others, one of the prophets."
>
> "But what about you?" he asked. "Who do you say I am?"
>
> Peter answered, "You are the Christ."
>
> Jesus warned them not to tell anyone about him.
>
> He then began to teach them that the Son of Man must suffer many things and be rejected by the elders, chief priests and teachers of the law, and that he must be killed and after three days rise again. (Mark 8:27-31)

Now by this point in the Gospels, to the knowing reader Jesus' identity is about as disguised as Clark Kent wearing glasses, but as we can tell from the story, it wasn't quite so intuitive to the disciples. And there was a good reason for that. Like the two enormous support structures of the Golden Gate Bridge jutting above the fog line in San Francisco Bay, the Old Testament contained two distinct portraits of the Messiah: one painting him as a powerful and victorious coming king, and the other revealing him as a humble and broken servant, suffering for the sins of his people. That they were connected was not in doubt, but *how* lay veiled beneath the fog. Take a look at the two portraits:

> In my vision at night I looked, and there before me was one like a son of man, coming with the clouds of heaven. He approached the Ancient of Days and was led into his presence. He was given authority, glory and sovereign power; all peoples, nations and men of every language worshiped him. His dominion is an everlasting dominion that will not pass away, and his kingdom is one that will never be destroyed. (Daniel 7:13-14)

> We all, like sheep, have gone astray,
>   each of us has turned to his own way;
> and the LORD has laid on him
>   the iniquity of us all.
> He was oppressed and afflicted,
>   yet he did not open his mouth;
> he was led like a lamb to the slaughter,
>   and as a sheep before her shearers is silent,
>   so he did not open his mouth. (Isaiah 53:6-7)

Only now that the disciples understood his true identity could Jesus explain the connection, overlaying the two images. At first glance, the resulting collage is about as intelligible as a Salvador Dali painting or a Beck album cover, but shapes and colors assembled in place as Jesus gave this basic explanation: "I am the messianic King, but the kingdom will be ushered in not through power and glory but through my suffering, rejection and death as I offer my life as a sacrifice for the sins of human-kind. Then, when the Son of God returns, he will return in power and glory." Two images, two comings, same Messiah.

With this clarified, Jesus' ministry moved with deliberate speed and intentionality toward a standing appointment with Pontius Pilate: "As the time approached for him to be taken up to heaven, Jesus resolutely set out for Jerusalem" (Luke 9:51).

In this last tour of ministry—en route to Jerusalem—there would be final warnings to Israel, increased conflict with the religious leaders, and last-minute instruction and preparation of the disciples.

The Growing Threat of Divine Abandonment

When one of those at the table with him heard this, he said to Jesus, "Blessed is the man who will eat at the feast in the kingdom of God."

Jesus replied: "A certain man was preparing a great banquet and invited many guests. At the time of the banquet he sent his servant to tell those who had been invited, 'Come, for everything is now ready.'

"But they all alike began to make excuses. The first said, 'I have just bought a field, and I must go and see it. Please excuse me.'

"Another said, 'I have just bought five yoke of oxen, and I'm on my way to try them out. Please excuse me.'

"Still another said, 'I just got married, so I can't come.'

"The servant came back and reported this to his master. Then the owner of the house became angry and ordered his servant, 'Go out quickly into the streets and alleys of the town and bring in the poor, the crippled, the blind and the lame.'

"'Sir,' the servant said, 'what you ordered has been done, but there is still room.'

"Then the master told his servant, 'Go out to the roads and country lanes and make them come in, so that my house will be full. I tell you, not one of those men who were invited will get a taste of my banquet.'" (Luke 14:15-24)

In 1975, Howard Johnson was the premiere outpost of upscale fast food in the United States. There were more than a thousand Howard Johnson restaurants zippering the American roadside. If only Howard Johnson could have foreseen the future: pitchforks, license plates and other barnyard trash nailed to restaurant walls, waiters as birthday-singing troubadours. If only. While the Howard Johnson hotel chain still survives, there are but five remaining HoJo restaurants. Yes sir, if things had been different, I'd be staring at a Howard Johnson restaurant on Route 100 near my house, instead of an Applebennigans. But they're not, so I'm not. Which is all by way of introducing the question: What if Israel had accepted Jesus as its Messiah? What if things had been different?

It would seem from a straightforward reading of the Old Testament that most Jews would have pictured the messianic plan unfolding something like this: When the Messiah came, he would vindicate Israel and judge the bullying nations that had mistreated her. Justice would come to the Middle Eastern playground, and detentions would be handed out accordingly. The many Jews who had been scattered and taken captive to other lands would return to Israel in a glorious home-coming. The message of the Messiah and his kingdom would go out to the world, the red carpet first unfurling in Israel and then rolling out to the nations. The Messiah would rule the nations from Israel, and the world would enjoy a golden age of peace, perhaps best pictured in the closing scene of *The Lord of the Rings: The Return of the King* when Aragorn is crowned king, or in the U2 song "I Still Haven't Found What I'm Looking For," where all the colors bleed into one. Both, incidentally, were meant as allusions to the messianic kingdom.

But the story Jesus told of the "great banquet" was a veiled threat—if you can refer to the statement "not one of those men who were invited will get a taste of my banquet" as being veiled (Luke 14:24). The Landlord was warning of an impending eviction notice. If Israel would not repent and receive her Messiah, the kingdom would open, but under new management. The message of the King and his kingdom would bypass Israel, and invitations would be sent instead to the Gentile nations—"out to the roads and country lanes," as referenced in the parable—where it would find a willing audience. In the end, Israel might reject its Messiah but would not be allowed to boycott the kingdom's grand opening.

As Jesus headed toward Jerusalem, on the last leg of his ministry, warnings to the nation of Israel increased: Cease and desist from your current course of faithlessness, or face the consequences. Alongside these warnings were growing implications that the next destination for the kingdom message would be the Gentiles and the nations beyond Israel's borders.

Intensifying Conflict with the Keepers of the Law

> On one occasion an expert in the law stood up to test Jesus. "Teacher," he asked, "what must I do to inherit eternal life?"
>
> "What is written in the Law?" he replied. "How do you read it?"
>
> He answered: "'Love the Lord your God with all your heart and with all your soul and with all your strength and with all your mind'; and, 'Love your neighbor as yourself.' "

"You have answered correctly," Jesus replied. "Do this and you will live."

But he wanted to justify himself, so he asked Jesus, "And who is my neighbor?"

In reply Jesus said: "A man was going down from Jerusalem to Jericho, when he fell into the hands of robbers. They stripped him of his clothes, beat him and went away, leaving him half dead. A priest happened to be going down the same road, and when he saw the man, he passed by on the other side. So too, a Levite, when he came to the place and saw him, passed by on the other side. But a Samaritan, as he traveled, came where the man was; and when he saw him, he took pity on him. He went to him and bandaged his wounds, pouring on oil and wine. Then he put the man on his own donkey, took him to an inn and took care of him. The next day he took out two silver coins and gave them to the inn-keeper. 'Look after him,' he said, 'and when I return, I will reimburse you for any extra expense you may have.'

"Which of these three do you think was a neighbor to the man who fell into the hands of robbers?" (Luke 10:25-36)

Radio station 103.5 is forever playing the Police's "Every Breath You Take," which is why I generally listen to 102.5. (Now your mental iPod will have no choice but to replay Sting's raspy voice—I'm really sorry about that.) In an interview Sting made the comment "Everyone thinks it's a love ballad, but it's actually an insidious little song about jealousy."[1]

Similar confusion is attached to this story of the Good Samaritan. It's an endearing story we tell children about what it means to be a good neighbor. One could almost picture Jesus slipping on his sneakers and sweater while he told it. But Jesus was not Mr. Rogers, and his stories were about as cheery and benign as *Hotel Rwanda*. No, this little tale is actually a chest-poking rebuke of Israel's nationalism and heartless legalism, for the hero of the story is not Israel's religious elite but a despised Samaritan.

If you locate Israel on a map, you will notice something significant: it sits on the tiny ligament of land that connects two enormous landmasses (Africa and Eurasia), like the Jersey Turnpike between New York and Philadelphia. This is no accident. God wanted Israel to be "a light on a hill," the only rest stop on the only turnpike. He wanted people from all over the known world to witness what it looked like when a nation followed God. He wanted all nations to come and know the one true God, and he wanted to use Israel as his calling card—or "rest stop," for metaphoric consistency.

But rather than inviting others to come and "know the Lord," Israel grew ethnocentric, that universal crazy glue that cements citizens together through shared prejudice and an us-versus-them mindset, keeping the borders garrisoned and always patrolling for illegal aliens (an attitude equally observable among Christian and Muslim communities). Their prayers to God were not for the redemption of the nations but for their extinction. While there were obviously individual exceptions, Israel as a whole failed to fulfill her role in God's global plan of redemption, and the prejudice of nationalism was to blame.

A caste system may be the most helpful construct for understanding the animosity of Jews toward Samaritans in the first century. Samaritans were Jews who had intermarried and mingled with those of other nations and were viewed as a combination of half-breed and trailer trash. Jews would not speak to them, make eye contact or let their shadow cross a Samaritan's path, and if they had to pass through Samaritan territory, they would shake the Samaritan dust off themselves before resuming the trip.

In the story it is the Samaritan who truly loves his neighbor. That doesn't sound like the insulting kick in the groin that it was, for the essence of the Mosaic Law could be distilled down to this phrase: "Love the Lord your God with all your heart, soul, and strength, and love your neighbor as yourself" (Mark 12:33). While the priest and Levite in the story went to great lengths to observe the letter of the law, they had left its spirit and intent stranded on the roadside. Jesus wasn't simply ranking the Samaritan as a better neighbor but rather portraying him as more obedient to the Law of Moses.

So the correct answer to Jesus' question of who was the better neighbor is B, the Samaritan. That answer would not have received a rousing endorsement by any of the Levites or priests sprinkled through the crowd. You can tell seditious little stories for only so long until people wise up and say, "Hey, I think he's talking about us." And of course he was.

During his ministry, Jesus had to contend with several political, potentially homicidal realities. Israel under Roman occupation was parceled out to several rulers.

The region of Judea, which contained the city of Jerusalem, was ruled by Rome, through the governance of Pontius Pilate. Historical sources show Pilate to have been a ruthless governor, quashing civil unrest in any form with cruel and unusual punishment.

To the north was the region of Galilee, where Rome had installed a Jewish client king by the name of Herod. His corruption and political paranoia had led to the execution of Israel's foremost prophet, John the Baptist.

The third castle on this political chessboard represents the religious powers, the chief priests and Pharisees, whose base of operations was Jerusalem. The oligarchy of priests ran the Temple in Jerusalem and thus controlled the sacramental and worship life of Israel, while the Pharisees maintained controlling interest in the synagogue system and thus the study and teaching of the Torah. It was most likely from Jerusalem that Pharisees were dispatched to monitor the subversive activities of Jesus.

With these land mines carefully marked on the map, and with our reporters embedded among the troops, we can glimpse the rationale behind Jesus' tactical maneuvers and serpentine movements across the countryside. For instance, when Jesus' popularity swelled in Galilee to the degree that the crowds tried to forcibly make him king (John 6:15), he immediately withdrew from the region and did not publicly appear there again. If he had, Herod would probably have killed him as he did John the Baptist. Jesus' insertions into Jerusalem were followed by swift retreats before civil war broke out and Pilate began firing on the crowds. In dealing with the Pharisees, Jesus didn't run from conflict but showed restraint, with his harshest critiques cushioned through third-person parables. But as Jesus moved toward his death, his confrontations brimmed with a bring-it-on tenacity. His rebukes of the religious leaders become less veiled and several decibels louder: "You snakes! You brood of vipers!" (Matthew 23:33). The leaders' tolerance of him, in turn, grew increasingly thin. A final showdown was brewing, and Jerusalem would become Jesus' last stand.

Premonitions of Death
Coming More Rapidly

Jesus took the Twelve aside and told them, "We are going up to Jerusalem, and everything that is written by the prophets about the Son of Man will be fulfilled. He will be handed over to the Gentiles. They will mock him, insult him, spit on him, flog him and kill him. On the third day he will rise again."

The disciples did not understand any of this. Its meaning was hidden from them, and they did not know what he was talking about. (Luke 18:31-34)

Toward the end of the Gospels, as he stood before his accusers, Jesus uttered one phrase several times:

"So, Jesus, are you the Messiah?"

"It is as you say."

A peculiar phrase, when you think about it. It seems to carry the meaning "I refuse to defend myself, nor will I put words in your mouth." The point, I think, is that by their own volition individuals were choosing to reject, betray and crucify Jesus. No one put words in anyone's mouth. Luke's Gospel underscores that Jesus' death was part of God's plan—in fact the very purpose for which he came. And yet no one's actions were coerced. I'm sure there is a theorem somewhere that explains how this can be, but for now we have a more important question to answer: Why did Jesus have to die at all?

I need to say up front that I think the answer is deeper than any answer I'll provide. It's like my wife asking me why I love her. I'm sure I could fill a page with reasons—I had *better* be able to fill a page with reasons—but in all honesty, the truth in its unimaginable complexity would never find its full expression there. That being said, think of what follows like the male and female icons over public restrooms: they are not anatomically or psychologically to human scale, but they communicate some general principles of great importance.

Let's begin with perfume. The expensive stuff is often made with ambergris, which is really rancid whale vomit (indigestible stuff whales periodically belch up) that's been floating around the ocean for who knows how long. In the perfume industry, ambergris is more valuable by the pound than gold or platinum, and as the story goes, the chief perfumer for Dior went to check out a thirty-kilo wad that had just been found washed up on shore. After handling the vile paste, he washed his hands, using the generic bar of soap sitting on the sink in the men's room. A few hours later, upon smelling his hands, he discovered Dioressence, which became one of Dior's all-time best-selling perfumes.[2] And all it really is, is the unusual mixture of soap and vomit—but it smells great on you, really.

To say that God is pure and holy is to state the obvious, but the Bible uses a far less expected word to describe the reaction when God's purity is brought into contact with sin and evil. That word is "vomit" (Leviticus 20:22; Revelation 3:16).[3] What happens when you drink poison? Typically you throw up. It's a natural reaction to a dangerous toxin or something the body finds injurious to itself.

God's innate reaction to evil, flowing from his purity, is to vomit it, destroy it, purge it—the sort of convulsive reaction you'd have upon finding a snake under your pillow or learning that your favorite perfume is made of whale vomit.

Now, this might not be a problem if you and I weren't riddled with the toxins, but we are. As illustrative of the point, at this very moment I count twenty-six wars going on in the world, along with genocide and other atrocities of which we are both aware. On a personal level, since 8:00 this morning I have envied, lied, hated, lusted and spent $15.50 on lunch and Starbucks that could have saved a child from starving. Or as the character Tyler Durden observes in the film *Fight Club:* "Murder, crime, poverty, these things don't concern me. What concerns me are celebrity magazines, television with 500 channels, some guy's name on my underwear."

I hope the contours of the dilemma that precipitated the death of Christ are beginning to emerge. God truly does love us, and he created us for the very purpose of loving us. And while it is true to say that God is love, it is also simplistic. God is also pure and holy (think soap), and therefore sin presents a major obstacle in our relationship with him (think vomit). I suppose God could just forget about our sin, but I don't think he can simply lop off attributes or qualities of himself, including his sin-repulsed holiness. God, while possessing all the attributes of love, justice, purity and holiness, is never in conflict with himself, and everything he does is consistent with all that he is.

It's in Christ's death that God is able to simultaneously love, forgive and destroy evil and sin. As the Scriptures phrase this bottomless mystery, "God made him who had no sin to be sin for us, so that in him we might become the righteousness of God" (2 Corinthians 5:21).

Perhaps this is too philosophical and abstract. If we were to try to put it into simpler language, it might go something like this:

All sin is spiritual garbage, and necessarily meets its end in destruction. God can't let garbage into heaven. Only if the "sinner" won't let go of his garbage does he get burned with it. God offers to take the garbage off his back, to separate the "sinner" from the sin so that the sinner is not separated from God. Jesus is the garbage man.[4]

You might expect the redemption of humankind to be more miraculous, more philosophically sophisticated, and instead here we are looking at a rejected Messiah, tortured beyond recognition, giving his life for ours. But God chose this apparent irony and foolishness to be the most fitting vehicle for the redemption of a terminally faithless and prideful humanity. The apostle Paul offers that disclaimer in his letter to the Corinthians:

Since in the wisdom of God the world through its wisdom did not know him, God was pleased through the foolishness of what was preached to save those who believe. Jews demand miraculous signs and Greeks look for wisdom, but we preach Christ crucified:

a stumbling block to Jews and foolishness to Gentiles. . . . For the foolishness of God is wiser than man's wisdom, and the weakness of God is stronger than man's strength. (1 Corinthians 1:21-23, 25)

The Gospel writers desperately wanted the reader to hear the message "God loves you, and it is for you, personally, that Christ died." In Jesus' waning months, he would revisit the topic of his impending death on several occasions, acclimating the disciples and preparing their systems to absorb the bodily shock.

The Ugly Alternative
Becoming More Inevitable

When the Son of Man comes in his glory, and all the angels with him, he will sit on his throne in heavenly glory. All the nations will be gathered before him, and he will separate the people one from another as a shepherd separates the sheep from the goats. He will put the sheep on his right and the goats on his left.

Then the King will say to those on his right, "Come, you who are blessed by my Father; take your inheritance, the kingdom prepared for you since the creation of the world. For I was hungry and you gave me something to eat, I was thirsty and you gave me something to drink, I was a stranger and you invited me in, I needed clothes and you clothed me, I was sick and you looked after me, I was in prison and you came to visit me."

Then the righteous will answer him, "Lord, when did we see you hungry and feed you, or thirsty and give you something to drink? When did we see you a stranger and invite you in, or needing clothes and clothe you? When did we see you sick or in prison and go to visit you?"

The King will reply, "I tell you the truth, whatever you did for one of the least of these brothers of mine, you did for me."

Then he will say to those on his left, "Depart from me, you who are cursed, into the eternal fire prepared for the devil and his angels. For I was hungry and you gave me nothing to eat, I was thirsty and you gave me nothing to drink, I was a stranger and you did not invite me in, I needed clothes and you did not clothe me, I was sick and in prison and you did not look after me."

They also will answer, "Lord, when did we see you hungry or thirsty or a stranger or needing clothes or sick or in prison, and did not help you?"

He will reply, "I tell you the truth, whatever you did not do for one of the least of these, you did not do for me."

Then they will go away to eternal punishment, but the righteous to eternal life. (Matthew 25:31-46)

Up to this point, Jesus' stern warnings for rejection were primarily corporate, national and temporal, referring to what would become of Israel if they rejected the Messiah. But here things suddenly get personal. What becomes of the individual who flips the finger toward heaven and rejects all divine attempts at reconciliation?

In 1915, George Burdick, city editor for the *New York Tribune,* broke the law by disobeying a court order requiring him to reveal his "undisclosed" news sources. President Woodrow Wilson, however, declared a full pardon for Burdick, clearing him of all offenses and crimes committed. Nothing too unusual up to this point. What made Burdick's case historic is that he refused the pardon. Burdick's refusal brought the case to the U.S. Supreme Court, which sided with Burdick, stating that a presidential pardon could not be forced on anyone.

If you went into the Gospels with a mental picture of Jesus as *Simp-*

sons neighbor Ned Flanders, a passage like Jesus' words in Matthew 25 will hit you like your grandmother dropping the "F" bomb. To understand the dissonance in Jesus' tone, keep in mind the variance of culture. Jesus is not an American or a Republican or a suburbanite. For any number of reasons, that's just good to remember. In the Louvre museum in Paris, you'll find dozens of "Jesus paintings" from the Renaissance. In the Italian paintings Jesus looks like Super Mario. In the paintings from the northern Renaissance he looks more Germanic, kind of like hall of fame quarterback Troy Aikman. It's just as easy to paint Jesus as an American (which he was not). So to see Jesus clearly, we need to take off our cultural glasses, or at least be aware that we're wearing them.

In keeping with the Jewish culture, Jesus commonly employed a rabbinic style of teaching (he is actually addressed several times in the Gospels as "Rabbi"), which among other things made frequent use of hyperbole, blasting out exaggerated statements meant to underscore a point, such as "It is easier for a camel to go through the eye of a needle than for a rich man to enter the kingdom of God" (Mark 10:25). In public address, Jesus purposefully spoke in a genre or manner meant to echo the Old Testament prophets. The prophets used terse, jolting, even sarcastic speech (*sarcasm* literally means "tearing of the flesh") in order to cut through the calloused hearts of their audience. All that to say, Jesus taught and spoke like a first-century Jew.

While we're on the subject of culture, try to keep in mind that today's dominant communication values of niceness, pleasantness, political correctness and all manner of oh-I-am-so-sorry-that's-my-bad sensitivities do not necessarily equate to love, care and compassion. These culturally preferred qualities are "voice tones," and like ring tones, they have little to do with the actual content of what we say and mean.

And so, unconcerned with twenty-first-century social faux pas and deaf to our nervous laughter, Jesus didn't shy away from uncomfortable topics. Of the twelve times the word *hell* is used in the New Testament, eleven are from the mouth of Jesus. And that makes sense, for if hell is real and Jesus knew of its reality—and eventuality for some—it would be hard to imagine why he wouldn't warn us of its danger.

As the Bible uses the metaphor of marriage to speak of our relationship with God, so hell is the ultimate "divorce." It is to be eternally separated from all light, love, goodness and joy—in other words, all that is God. Although one might want to disbelieve in hell for any number of reasons, there is a stern logic to it. If we were created with free will, then we possess the power to accept a relationship with God or the power— God help us—to decline it. C. S. Lewis laid out the logical necessity of this inverted spiritual existence.

> If the happiness of a creature lies in self surrender, no one can make that surrender but himself. . . . I would pay any price to be able to say truthfully "all will be saved." But my reason retorts, "With their will or without it?" If I say "Without their will," I at once perceive a contradiction; how can the supreme voluntary act of self-surrender be involuntary? If I say "With their will," my reason replies "How, if they will not give in?"[5]

Following this flow of reasoning, Lewis added, "I willingly believe that the damned are, in one sense, successful, rebels to the end; that the doors of Hell are locked from the inside. . . . They enjoy forever the horrible freedom they have demanded."[6]

It's not divine determinism that creates hell; it's human agency—the free and willful choice to reject God. To say that free will exists is to say that hell must as well. As G. K. Chesterton put it, "Hell is the greatest compliment God has ever paid to the dignity of human freedom." I mean, if heaven is a place of compassion, joy, self-giving love, surrender, humility, kindness, worship, and truth, you have to stop and consider that you probably know several people who flat-out wouldn't like it there!

We haven't hitherto discussed flames, pitchforks or mine shafts delving into the earth's core (this is also our first use of the word *hitherto*). To say that hell exists is one thing; to say what it's like is quite another. Jesus' descriptions are vague and metaphoric, referring to "outer darkness" and "eternal fire" (Matthew 25:30, 41). As darkness and flames are mutually exclusive, I don't think he was trying to describe its architecture. "Darkness" in all likelihood reflects the exclusion of everything that is God, including light, with "flames" speaking of passions and desires unfulfilled and fanned out of control—a state of being consumed by desire. It is in this sense that hell is not parallel to heaven at all. To quote Lewis for what I promise to be the last time, "To enter heaven is to become more human than you ever succeeded in being in earth; to enter hell, is to be banished from humanity . . . to consist of a will utterly centered in its self and passions utterly uncontrolled by the will. It is of course, impossible to imagine."[7]

Final Instructions
Becoming More Urgent

An argument started among the disciples as to which of them would be the greatest. Jesus, knowing their thoughts, took a little child and had him stand beside him. Then he said to them, "Whoever welcomes this little child in my name welcomes me; and whoever welcomes me welcomes the one who sent me. For he who is least among you all—he is the greatest."

"Master," said John, "we saw a man driving out demons in your name and we tried to stop him, because he is not one of us."

"Do not stop him," Jesus said, "for whoever is not against you is for you."

As the time approached for him to be taken up to heaven, Jesus resolutely set out for Jerusalem. And he sent messengers on ahead, who went into a Samaritan village to get things ready for him; but the people there did not welcome him, because he was heading for Jerusalem. When the disciples James and John saw this, they asked, "Lord, do you want us to call fire down from heaven to destroy them?" But Jesus turned and rebuked them, and they went to another village. (Luke 9:46-56)

As Jesus headed toward Jerusalem, pressing squarely on the front of his mind, and bringing tension to his lower jaw and perhaps causing him to grind his teeth, was the state of preparedness of his disciples. The baton would be passed to them, and as he looked at his relay partners, what he saw was not exactly a sleek squad of sprinters. And while he might have been concerned with any number of rough edges in the disciples, his focus was primarily on one: the problem of power.

The Jewish religious leaders, like most religious leaders throughout history, had created a two-tiered spiritual caste system, separating those in the spiritual know from those who knew next to nothing. Power resides in knowledge, and so the trick is to keep it to yourself, not allowing anyone to peek at the hand you're playing. You would think that such down-to-earth, blue-collar, working stiffs as the disciples would be immune to this, but no one is immune to this, because, as they say, power corrupts and absolute power corrupts absolutely. And in these stories we see that corruption had already begun to erode the foundation of the incipient church, that is, the disciples.

In the first incident (Luke 9:46-48), the disciples had begun to jockey for position, titles, bonuses and perks on the kingdom's corporate ladder. They each wanted the corner office next to Jesus. They were ambitious for power.

In the second incident (Luke 9:49-50), we see that they had become competitive not only with each other but also with other ministries. Someone else was doing the work of the kingdom, but that person was not them, so he had to be stopped—who did he think he was? They began to feel a need to fight for greater market share and viewership and to monopolize the ministry of the kingdom.

In the third incident (Luke 9:51-56), the disciples had assumed that the authority to proclaim the gospel gave them the right to dispense judgment. It did not. Judgment is the prerogative of God alone, Having greedily elbowed out competitors as well as each other in a grab for power, here they were effectively trying to tug power away from God himself.

These stories, compressed together like a three-car pileup, feel to me like the Mount Doom scene toward the end of *The Lord of the Rings: The Return of the King*. After seventy-two hours of viewing, you come to love and empathize with Frodo in his struggles to resist the "ring of power." So when his face turns sinister and he slips the ring on his finger, succumbing to its seduction, you want to yell out, "Nooooooo!" Who knows, but maybe Jesus felt this way as he witnessed the corruption and moral failure of those he had invested his life in, those who had heard his repeated condemnations of religious hypocrisy.

Both the problem and Jesus' rebuke would be repeated several times on the way to Jerusalem. If Jesus was discouraged, he didn't show it. Instead he persistently modeled for his disciples the meaning of servant leadership, giving it its ultimate definition through his suffering and death. He would hearse and rehearse with them the inverted principles of the kingdom's corporate structure: "If anyone wants to be first, he must be the very last, and the servant of all" (Mark 9:35). This would need to go on every coffee mug and piece of stationery in the office. The top criteria for leadership within the kingdom would be humility, sacrificial service and servanthood, and the genius of this business plan was that it was a corrective—the only corrective—against the corruption of power: to give power away.

As is not surprising, Jesus' foresight about the problem of power, corruption and hypocrisy within his disciples was well founded. Even if the first generation learned the lesson from their mistakes, many in the history of the church have forgotten it. In fact, this problem is responsible for the most devastating split in church history, the Reformation.

In 1516, a scholar and media darling of the sixteenth century, Erasmus, published an edition of the original Greek text of the New Testament, with a fresh Latin translation. Upon reading the New Testament in the Greek, Martin Luther realized that the Church's interpretation of Matthew 4:17—"Do penance, [for the kingdom of heaven is near]," which involved paying indulgences to Rome—was inaccurate. The text actually says, "Repent," referring to a change of heart and having no connection whatsoever to one's wallet.[8] This, among other things, led to a string of thoughts in Luther's mind that went something like this: "The Church is hoarding power through keeping people ignorant of the Scriptures. The Church has used that power to funnel money to itself. The Church has been corrupted through power and greed. This sounds like those three stories of the disciples in Luke 9:46-56."

If you think Martin Luther was the only one aware of the corruption, or the only one pushing for reform, you're mistaken. Many within the Church at the time also wanted reform. Whether Luther pushed too hard, the Church moved too slow or those in power would not concede isn't the point. The point is this: the greatest division in Christian history might have been avoided simply by learning from this text, learning from the disciples' failure, learning from Jesus' warning.

Oh, the other stories we could tell. But we won't, because someone else's failure, someone else's hypocrisy, too easily becomes an excuse for our own spiritual lethargy. I mean, it is inexcusable what certain people, churches, and institutions have done through the ages under the banner of Christianity. It just isn't an excuse.

The Gospel of Mark provides us with a snapshot capturing the emotion of Jesus' last tour of duty; he mentions back-to-back the only two occurrences of Jesus "sighing" in the Gospels.

> There some people brought to him a man who was deaf and could hardly talk, and they begged him to place his hand on the man. He looked up to heaven and with a deep sigh said to him, "*Ephphatha!*" (which means, "Be opened!"). At this, the man's ears were opened, his tongue was loosened and he began to speak plainly. (Mark 7:32, 34-35)
>
> The Pharisees came and began to question Jesus. To test him, they asked him for a sign from heaven. He sighed deeply and said, "Why does this generation ask for a miraculous sign? I tell you the truth, no sign will be given to it." (Mark 8:11,12)

In the repetition of "sighs" we get the sense that Jesus' had grown weary of beating his head against a wall. The endless streams of broken bodies and lives, the dullness of his disciples, the incessant antagonism and disbelief of the religious leaders: "When will it end?" Tragically, very soon.

5   SCAPEGOAT

The Death of Innocence

The Western world runs on time; comprehension is contingent on the establishment of chronology. You can't watch an episode of *24* or *Lost* without knowing the hour of the day or the number of days on the island. The Eastern world has never paid such homage to time and would be appalled, I'm sure, by how many times a day we turn our prayer mats in the direction of the clock. The Gospels employ an assortment of organizing themes other than chronology, never reading, for example, "Day 17: Jesus walks on water." And yet, as Jesus' ministry comes down to the final week, the Gospels become extremely time-conscious.

On Sunday, Jesus rode into Jerusalem a celebrity, the crowds lauding him with praise and palm branches as Israel's Messiah. This only confirmed to the religious leaders the necessity of their assassination plot and the need for haste. On Monday and Tuesday, verbal gunfire erupted between Jesus and the religious leaders. Wednesday there was apparently a ceasefire, as the day is passed over in silence by the Gospels. On Thursday evening, Jesus celebrated Passover as the Last Supper with his disciples and then went to the Garden of Gethsemane to pray. It was here that Jesus was taken into custody. Through Thursday night and into Friday morning, Jesus was dragged through three mock trials: one before the religious leaders of the Sanhedrin, another before Herod the Jewish king of Israel (the region of Galilee, specifically), and then finally a third before the Roman governor Pontius Pilate. Friday afternoon, Jesus was crucified. His body was taken down and laid in a tomb early Friday evening. On Sunday came the first reports that the tomb was empty and that many had seen Jesus resurrected.

The Gospels are organized biographies compiled several decades after the events, drawing from the memorized teachings of Jesus, sermons and interviews by the original disciples, and written vignettes of events like the Last Supper or Crucifixion. While all of the key teachings of Jesus would have been memorized by the disciples, there is no reason not to conclude that at some point the most literate of their number, someone such as Matthew, wrote them down. In fact, someone probably did. The recorded "traditions," however (the arrival in Jerusalem, the trial before Pilate, etc.), were not memorized "teachings" but historic descriptions of key events. As such they were probably the first to be written down, perhaps within months and certainly within a couple of years of the events. As the final week, recorded in the Gospels, is primarily a series of these early historical vignettes, they are filled with the wonderful hallmarks of eyewitness details written down hurriedly after the event.

Here's a good example: "So Peter and the other disciple started for the tomb. Both were running, but the other disciple outran Peter and reached the tomb first" (John 20:3, 4). Apparently John ("the other disciple") felt that future generations should know that in a 100-yard sprint he could easily beat Peter. "Whatever else I tell you concerning the life of Jesus, just know this: I am twice as fast as my lethargic friend Peter. And don't you ever forget it." We can almost hear their "trash talk" echoing down through the ages, "I smoked you, man, I smoked you." So read these "last week" vignettes and appreciate them as eyewitness accounts of the last week of Jesus' earthly life, for that is assuredly what they are.

Peter's Nervous Breakdown

While they were eating, Jesus took bread, gave thanks and broke it, and gave it to his disciples, saying, "Take it; this is my body."

Then he took the cup, gave thanks and offered it to them, and they all drank from it.

"This is my blood of the covenant, which is poured out for many," he said to them. "I tell you the truth, I will not drink again of the fruit of the vine until that day when I drink it anew in the kingdom of God."

When they had sung a hymn, they went out to the Mount of Olives.

"You will all fall away," Jesus told them, "for it is written:

" 'I will strike the shepherd,

and the sheep will be scattered.'

But after I have risen, I will go ahead of you into Galilee."

Peter declared, "Even if all fall away, I will not."

"I tell you the truth," Jesus answered, "today—yes, tonight—before the rooster crows twice you yourself will disown me three times."

But Peter insisted emphatically, "Even if I have to die with you, I will never disown you." And all the others said the same. (Mark 14:22-31)

While Peter was below in the courtyard, one of the servant girls of the high priest came by. When she saw Peter warming himself, she looked closely at him.

"You also were with that Nazarene, Jesus," she said.

But he denied it. "I don't know or understand what you're talking about," he said, and went out into the entryway.

When the servant girl saw him there, she said again to those standing around, "This fellow is one of them." Again he denied it.

After a little while, those standing near said to Peter, "Surely you are one of them, for you are a Galilean."

He began to call down curses on himself, and he swore to them, "I don't know this man you're talking about."

Immediately the rooster crowed the second time. Then Peter remembered the word Jesus had spoken to him: "Before the rooster crows twice you will disown me three times." And he broke down and wept. (Mark 14:66-72)

I'm guessing that in the history of Christendom a million sermons have been preached on Peter's indiscretion (I like to guess at things when there is no way to validate my accuracy). So we will begin by looking at a different point altogether.

I'm sure we've all heard of skeptics who accuse the Gospels of containing all manner of fabrications, placed there in blinded zeal by the disciples or other church leaders in order to strengthen the growing church or propagate the Christian faith. If this were true, you'd have to step back and ask, "Why would the Gospel writers make up damaging and humiliating facts such as Peter's denial?" Peter became the leading figure of the early church, to whom all turned for strength and direction. How, exactly, would it have been helpful to portray him in this way: "All hail Peter, denier of the Christ, disciple with neither spine nor backbone, friend to the weak and cowardly, traitor to the Most High"?

In fact, one of the major ways historians evaluate the accuracy of ancient documents is to look for counterproductive features; these are the hallmark not of myth or propaganda but of history. In other words, if you're reading an ancient Roman document and it describes Caligula as a compassionate, folksy, down-to-earth leader of the community, it's propaganda. If it describes him as a depraved, inbred, masochistic sociopath, then it's history. If the Gospels were anything but historical documents, you would never find this scandalous account of Peter's denial, nor would you find mention of any of the following:

- Jesus' last words are recorded as "My God, my God, why have you forsaken me?" (Matthew 27:46). If you were fabricating material and could create any last words for Jesus, is this really what you would choose?

- After Jesus' death, two women were the first to discover that his tomb was empty and to testify of this fact (Luke 23:55—24:11). But in patriarchal first-century Israel, a woman's testimony was not even admissible in court. Not very compelling.

- The disciples are portrayed in the Gospels as competitive, petty, status-seeking and generally dense (Luke 9:46-56). How does it help to characterize the leaders of the church this way?

- At one point, one of the Gospels mentions that Jesus' family members came to take hold of him, for they thought he had lost his mind (Mark 3:21). That's not very reassuring!

If you read through the Gospels with an eye for this particular feature, you'd be amazed by the shameless disclosure of unflattering and counterproductive details that are clearly the mark of history. Having noted Peter's denial the second detail of significance in this story is that Jesus seems to have known this history before it happened.

Jesus might have often known what was going to happen but simply kept such knowledge to himself. I don't struggle with bouts of omniscience, so I don't really know. But I do know why he offered a trailer of future events in this instance. In the insanity of these few days, it could seem, to the untrained eye, that all hell had broken loose and that humankind had been able to hijack the King and kingdom. Jesus' predictions were to assure, upon later reflection, that this was God-ordered anarchy, and that no one had taken the life of the Son of God; it had been voluntarily given. Yes, it certainly could seem like the worldly powers had staged a coup, overthrown the guards and stormed the palace, but nothing could be further from the truth, and Jesus' knowledge of what was to follow was an assurance that the plot against him would succeed not because of the brilliance of his enemies' plan but because their plan also happened to be his.

Though Jesus knew of Peter's impending denial, Peter's failure was his own. In a sense, Peter failed because Peter needed to fail. He claimed that, though all others might fall away, he never would. One of the most disastrous things that could have befallen Christianity is if Peter had kept that promise. In that case, the key figure of the early church would have continued to operate under the faulty proposition that radical commitment is the key to the Christian life. It is not. Radical grace is.

Everyone who comes to Christ is in need of mercy, forgiveness and empowerment to accomplish his will. Following Christ is something we do out of gratitude for mercy given and out of a sense that he has what we need to carry on. If Peter had gutted it out, he would have been a different person, seen Christ differently, seen himself differently. We would have found ancient scrolls from the first-century church reading "Suck it up" rather than the humbled sentiment of the Lord's Prayer: "Give us today our daily bread." Peter could have been Christianity's first motivational speaker. A Pharisee could have been leading the church. Thank God he failed. Jesus knew it all beforehand, then toasted to it.

As far as a passionate heart goes, Peter was the best of our species. Which is perhaps the strongest argument for why we needed a Messiah.

Pilate Washed His Hands
and Sealed His Fate

Pilate took Jesus and had him flogged. The soldiers twisted together a crown of thorns and put it on his head. They clothed him in a purple robe and went up to him again and again, saying, "Hail, king of the Jews!" And they struck him in the face.

Once more Pilate came out and said to the Jews, "Look, I am bringing him out to you to let you know that I find no basis for a charge against him." When Jesus came out wearing the crown of thorns and the purple robe, Pilate said to them, "Here is the man!"

As soon as the chief priests and their officials saw him, they shouted, "Crucify! Crucify!"

But Pilate answered, "You take him and crucify him. As for me, I find no basis for a charge against him."

The Jews insisted, "We have a law, and according to that law he must die, because he claimed to be the Son of God."

When Pilate heard this, he was even more afraid, and he went back inside the palace. "Where do you come from?" he asked Jesus, but Jesus gave him no answer. "Do you refuse to speak to me?" Pilate said. "Don't you realize I have power either to free you or to crucify you?"

Jesus answered, "You would have no power over me if it were not given to you from above. Therefore the one who handed me over to you is guilty of a greater sin."

From then on, Pilate tried to set Jesus free, but the Jews kept shouting, "If you let this man go, you are no friend of Caesar. Anyone who claims to be a king opposes Caesar."

When Pilate heard this, he brought Jesus out and sat down on the judge's seat at a place known as the Stone Pavement (which in Aramaic is Gabbatha). It was the day of Preparation of Passover Week, about the sixth hour.

"Here is your king," Pilate said to the Jews.

But they shouted, "Take him away! Take him away! Crucify him!"

"Shall I crucify your king?" Pilate asked.

"We have no king but Caesar," the chief priests answered.

Finally Pilate handed him over to them to be crucified. (John 19:1-16)

The historicity of Pontius Pilate is a case study in the current trends of archaeology. It wasn't long ago that critics questioned the existence of Pilate because of little corroboration from historical documents. But in June of 1961, while excavating an ancient Roman amphitheater near Caesarea, archaeologists uncovered an enormous limestone block bearing an inscription that dedicated the structure to Tiberius Caesar. Naturally, part of the inscription named the person who had dedicated it. It read, "Pontius Pilate, Prefect of Judea."[1]

This stone is part of a larger archipelago of recent discoveries confirming historical pieces of the New Testament:

- In Acts 18:12-17 we read how Paul was brought before Gallio, the proconsul of Achaia. At Delphi, an inscription of a letter from Emperor Claudius was discovered stating, "Lucius Junios Gallio, my friend, and the proconsul of Achaia."[2]

- Romans 16:23 names Erastus, a coworker of the apostle Paul, as the treasurer of the city of Corinth. Archaeologists excavating a Corinthian theater discovered an inscription that says, "Erastus in return for his aedilship [appointment to public office] laid the pavement at his own expense." The pavement was laid in A.D. 50.[3]

- In John 5:1-15 we find the story of how Jesus healed a man at the Pool of Bethesda. John described the pool as having five porticoes.

This site had been in dispute until recently, forty feet under the surface of the present city, archaeologists discovered a pool with five porticoes.[4]

And the list of discoveries goes on. One prominent archaeologist examined Luke's references of thirty-two countries, fifty-four cities, nine islands and key historical figures. He didn't find a single mistake.[5]

I'm not sure what my point in all this was. Perhaps it was that every person, in his or her lifetime, should go on an archaeological dig. Or maybe it was a plea to preserve our natural resources. No, I don't think that was it. Oh yes, the historicity of Pilate.

Pilate was the Roman governor in Judea. Israel was a conquered territory, and while maintaining a strong degree of indigenous leadership, it still wobbled on the puppet strings of Rome. As Rome did not want to supply arms to local vigilantes or insurrectionists, the Roman governor alone had the power to execute capital punishment, and so it was inevitable that the case of Jesus would bounce its way into Pilate's court.

The etymology of the Greek word used in the Bible for "sincerity" or "transparency" literally means "judged by the sun,"[6] the opposite of which is duplicity: having hidden motives and agendas. It's a word picture meaning, that when you bring something out into broad daylight, all mysteries vanish, veneer is stripped away, and reality is laid bare. Pilate's encounter with Jesus seems to have had this glaring effect, and what we witness is a heart starkly divided, allegiances cubicled like office space—a lack of sincerity and integrity.

On the one hand, Pilate had a bloodthirsty mob trolling the waters like sharks awaiting a man overboard. Jesus, however, had masses of supporters, and Pilate did not want a riot or civil war, as his role in Israel was to prevent them. Add to that the political pressure exerted by the local Jewish leaders (the Sanhedrin), and a recent Roman mandate ordering him to make all efforts to accommodate them.[7] But there was not only pressure from below on the organizational chart; there was also pressure from above. Jesus had claimed authority (to be the King of the Jews) reserved for Caesar alone, and failure to make an example out of him would not play well in Rome, meaning Pilate's next job might be janitor at the Colosseum.

None of this would have been such a problem if it were not for the nagging sense that his prisoner might actually be who he claimed to be—the Son of God. In a personal interrogation of Jesus, Pilate sought to intimidate and assert his authority—"Don't you realize I have power either to free you or to crucify you?"—but as the interview progressed, he had all he could do to maintain eye contact and a firm handshake. Despite Jesus' appearance of absolute vulnerability and weakness, Pilate sensed an intrinsic power and authority that made him squirm and left him questioning everything: his senses, his intuition, his beliefs, his life.

Indecision is usually rooted in one of two things: either you're not sure what the right decision is or you *do* know but you lack the moral courage to act on it. In this case, the evidence would argue for the latter. Pilate refused to make a decision about Jesus, and attempted to wash his hands of the responsibility.

But history did not afford Pilate that option. In the end, I'm not sure it will afford any of us that option. There really are moments and issues in life where a failure to act, decide or cast a vote is to, in effect, have voted in the negative. According to the Gospels, our decision about the Messiah is one of them. We will all find ourselves at some point sitting in the seat of Pilate, having to weigh repurcusions and implications, having to decide about Jesus. For Pilate, the demands of the masses, of Rome, of his career and of his reputation ultimately drowned out the whispers of his conscience. He consented to the demands of the people: "Finally Pilate handed [Jesus] over to them to be crucified" (John 19:16).

The lack of Jesus' supporters within the rancorous crowd can be attributed to the smaller public hearing set within the precincts of the military barracks, with a crowd hand-picked by the chief priests. As befitting Pilate's lack of sincerity and integrity, the entire judicial operation did not take place in the full light of day, but rather before a sleeping Jerusalem was even aware of what had transpired. By 9:00 a.m., Jesus had been tried, condemned and crucified.

Jesus: Good and Dead

Knowing that all was now completed, and so that the Scripture would be fulfilled, Jesus said, "I am thirsty." A jar of wine vinegar was there, so they soaked a sponge in it, put the sponge on a stalk of the hyssop plant, and lifted it to Jesus' lips. When he had received the drink, Jesus said, "It is finished." With that, he bowed his head and gave up his spirit.

Now it was the day of Preparation, and the next day was to be a special Sabbath. Because the Jews did not want the bodies left on the crosses during the Sabbath, they asked Pilate to have the legs broken and the bodies taken down. The soldiers therefore came and broke the legs of the first man who had been crucified with Jesus, and then those of the other. But when they came to Jesus and found that he was already dead, they did not break his legs. Instead, one of the soldiers pierced Jesus' side with a spear, bringing a sudden flow of blood and water. The man who saw it has given testimony, and his testimony is true. He knows that he tells the truth, and he testifies so that you also may believe. (John 19:28-35)

As unfathomable as this may be, the following is a message from an ac-

tual website: "The moon landing was faked. John Glenn, Neil Armstrong
and whoever else was involved in the moon mission never actually left
earth. They filmed all of the moon footage in a sound studio in Burbank,
California."

The problem with paranoia is not that it's illogical; it's that the circle
of logic is obsessively small:

"You work for the CIA."

"No, I don't."

"The CIA always deny it."

One of the beliefs behind revisionist stories such as *The Da Vinci
Code*—and Islam, for that matter—is that Jesus didn't really die on the
cross. But while we don't possess many writings from first- and second-
century historians, what we do have makes Jesus' death a certainty.

- Lucian (A.D. 120–180) referred to Jesus as a crucified sophist (phi-
  losopher).[8]

- Josephus (A.D. 37–100) wrote, "At this time there appeared Jesus, a
  wise man, for he was a doer of amazing deeds. When Pilate condemned him to the cross, the leading men among us, having accused
  him, those who loved him did not cease to do so."[9]

- Tacitus (A.D. 56–120) wrote, "Christus, from whom the name had its
  origin, suffered the extreme penalty . . . at the hands of our procurator
  Pontius Pilate."[10]

This is a bit like finding that the *New York Times, Chicago Tribune*
and *Washington Post* all listed Jesus in their obituaries: "Founder of
Christendom dies, leaves behind 11 close friends and one traitor." While
such corroboration is certainly affirming, a story from John's Gospel provides the evidence of an actual autopsy. John observed "blood and water" flowing from Jesus' body after a Roman soldier pierced his side with
a spear (John 19:34). John may have thought that this was either mirac-

ulous, religiously symbolic (water and blood typifying baptism and atonement), or—who knows?—maybe just plain creepy. Whatever he thought, it is doubtful that he had in mind the following facts: The "water" was almost certainly pericardium fluid, which is a clear liquid looking exactly like water. The blood was, well, blood. If Jesus' lung and heart had been pierced by the Roman spear, as most likely they were, this is exactly what you'd expect to find oozing from the side of Jesus: blood and watery pericardium fluid. Thus John gave us an inadvertent autopsy, absolutely reliable because that was not his intent.

John's forensic skills earned the approval by the American Medical Association, which went on record with the following statement: "Clearly, the weight of historical and medical evidence indicated that Jesus was dead; . . . the spear, thrust between His right ribs, probably perforated not only the right lung but also the pericardium and heart and thereby ensured His death."[11] Now, I'm not sure why the Association waited two thousand years to make such a statement, but maybe that explains why it took sixty years to get a medical endorsement that smoking causes cancer.

While the 2004 movie *The Passion of the Christ* might make the following description superfluous, and though it personally bothers me to think about it, we should review the particulars of the crucifixion nonetheless. Prior to being nailed to the cross, Jesus was beaten with a Roman cat-o'-nine-tails, a whip with bits of bone and metal that would tear the flesh and expose the muscles and even the bowels of the victim. Jesus was punched repeatedly, kicked and spit upon. Using mallets, the Roman executioners thumped heavy, square, wrought-iron nails through Jesus' wrists and feet into a wooden cross. Afterward they dropped the cross into a hole. Jesus hung on the cross for approximately six hours, from about 9:00 a.m. to 3:00 p.m., before crying out, "It is finished" and breathing his final breath.[12]

While today the importance of "last words" is to find out who's getting cut out of the family trust fund, in the ancient world "last words" were more weighty, endowed with profound significance. Matthew tells us that Jesus made two last utterances, and neither is trivial. The first, contained in both Mark and Matthew, is "My God, my God, why have you forsaken me?" In light of all I've said about the purpose of Jesus' death, his asking this question would seem to suggest that I have some serious explaining to do. Here's my explanation: Psalm 22.

My God, my God, why have you forsaken me?
    Why are you so far from saving me,
    so far from the words of my groaning? . . .
All who see me mock me;
    they hurl insults, shaking their heads:
"He trusts in the LORD;
    let the LORD rescue him.
Let him deliver him,
    since he delights in him." . . .
I am poured out like water,
    and all my bones are out of joint.
My heart has turned to wax;
    it has melted away within me.
My strength is dried up like a potsherd,
    and my tongue sticks to the roof of my mouth;
    you lay me in the dust of death.
Dogs have surrounded me;
    a band of evil men has encircled me,
    they have pierced my hands and my feet.
I can count all my bones;
    people stare and gloat over me.

They divide my garments among them
   and cast lots for my clothing.
But you, O LORD, be not far off;
   O my Strength, come quickly to help me. . . .
Posterity will serve him;
   future generations will be told about the Lord.
They will proclaim his righteousness
   to a people yet unborn—
   for he has done it. (Psalm 22:1, 7, 8, 14-19, 30, 31)

Though written by Israel's King David a thousand years before the events of Jesus' death, Psalm 22 sounds like it's describing Jesus' crucifixion doesn't it? It certainly makes sense, then, for Jesus to have quoted it on the cross. But it is also astounding how precisely Jesus' death enacted and fulfilled the words—David's suffering, clearly a prophetic echo of Christ's.

Jesus' final, final words—"It is finished"—may seem a demure endnote: a more mundane string of final words would be difficult to imagine. But in context it probably means something like "I have accomplished the redemption of the entire human race." If this is the case, then we are looking at the most significant three words ever spoken, as well as the greatest example of understatement in human history. And with these words, "he bowed his head and gave up his spirit" (John 19:30). John's account provides us with a statement of certainty, foundational to what is to follow.

The Rise of Jesus

Early on the first day of the week, while it was still dark, Mary Magdalene went to the tomb and saw that the stone had been removed from the entrance. So she came running to Simon Peter and the other disciple, the one Jesus loved, and said, "They have taken the Lord out of the tomb, and we don't know where they have put him!"

So Peter and the other disciple started for the tomb. Both were running, but the other disciple outran Peter and reached the tomb first. He bent over and looked in at the strips of linen lying there but did not go in. Then Simon Peter, who was behind him, arrived and went into the tomb. He saw the strips of linen lying there, as well as the burial cloth that had been around Jesus' head. The cloth was folded up by itself, separate from the linen. Finally the other disciple, who had reached the tomb first, also went inside. He saw and believed. (They still did not understand from Scripture that Jesus had to rise from the dead.) . . .

On the evening of that first day of the week, when the disciples were together, with the doors locked for fear of the Jews, Jesus came and stood among them and said, "Peace be with you!" After he said this, he showed them his hands and side. The disciples were overjoyed when they saw the Lord. (John 20:1-9, 19, 20)

I spent some years working in advertising—writing commercials, ads and yes (ashamedly) even jingles. (I actually only wrote one jingle which I had to sing to a boardroom full of clients—talk about feeling like a spanked butt.) The key to advertising, of course, is branding. The right tagline, logo, spokesperson, voice-over—all are essential elements in creating the image of a product. In my mind it is impossible to conceive of a better vehicle, a better symbol or analogy, for redemption and the gospel message than the resurrection. Its meaning is not simply that of "life" or "new life" or "creation," but it carries with it the nuance of meaning "life out of death": the power of God to transform death, evil and corruption into life. And so the resurrection stands as the hallmark, or tagline, of Jesus' ministry.

The veracity of Jesus' life and ministry stands or falls on the historical authenticity of this event, and so the issue to ponder is not so much the event itself as it is the evidence for the event. Was Jesus resurrected?

Historically, we know that Jesus was crucified to death, and we also know that his tomb was empty. Even the earliest polemics against Christianity accused the disciples of stealing the body, ergo, everyone agreed the tomb was empty. But what proof do we have for the resurrection? We'll follow four different lines of evidence, with the disclaimer that this is courtroom evidence, not scientific evidence. In a laboratory, evidence lies in replicating the event; in a courtroom, evidence proves the likelihood of a conclusion. And while it would be nice if Jesus were to appear again as you read this, I'm not making any promises.

The first line of evidence concerns the disciples. Having believed that Jesus was the Messiah, they were as shocked as anyone else to see him splayed on a Roman cross. This is not what anyone had pictured happening to Israel's Redeemer. For the disciples, his death induced fear of persecution, grief, discouragement and mental confusion ("Did we believe in the wrong guy?"). Peter Steinfels, in an article in the *New York Times,* raised the obvious issue: "Shortly after Jesus was executed, his followers were suddenly galvanized from a baffled and cowering group into people whose message about a living Jesus and a coming kingdom, preached at the risk of their lives, eventually changed an empire. Something happened. . . . But exactly what?"[13]

Eleven uneducated, unarmed fishermen and a rabbled handful of other followers literally conquered the Roman Empire. Such passion, conviction, motivation and transformation seem to defy any other explanation *except* a resurrection. Seriously, think about it. If they had stolen the body and the whole thing was just a massive lie, could this royal society of nobodies really have changed the entire world?

The second line of proof looks at the same fact but from a different angle. Eventually, nearly every one of the disciples was brutally martyred. Unzipping the body bags, we find the following: Andrew was martyred by crucifixion; Bartholomew was beaten and then crucified; James and Judas (not Iscariot) were stoned to death; Matthew was speared to death; Peter was crucified upside down; Phillip and Simon were both crucified; James was beheaded; Thomas was speared to death; and Mathias was stoned.[14]

What, then, did the disciples have to gain by lying about Jesus' resurrection? Every lie has a motive, right? Yet the disciples proclaimed his resurrection in full possession of the knowledge that it would cost them their lives. But it's actually more puzzling than that, for if the disciples knew that Jesus hadn't been resurrected, then they also knew he wasn't the true Messiah. They were, then, propagating a false messiah. In doing so, according to their own Jewish belief system, they were ensuring damnation.[15] So, imagine being sawed in half with something like, say, a tree stump, causing the procedure to take hours. At any time you can save your life, not to mention your bowels, and avoid hell if you simply recant. "Did I say he rose from the dead? I meant, 'He sure looked red.'" But the disciples didn't, and if they were lying, then we are desperately lacking a motive for it.

The third line of proof comes from Jesus. He once said, "A wicked and adulterous generation asks for a miraculous sign! But none will be given it except the sign of the prophet Jonah. For as Jonah was three days and three nights in the belly of a huge fish, so the Son of Man will be three days and three nights in the heart of the earth" (Matthew 12:39-40). Jesus authenticated his whole mission and ministry with the claim that he would rise from the dead. This is not the guy running the graveyard shift at the Seven-Eleven but the person whose moral teachings have altered humanity more than those of anyone who has ever existed, ever. Even his enemies admitted that he had performed miracles, and his life fulfilled every messianic prophecy contained in the Old Testament. Though the claim that he would rise from the dead was admittedly amazing, you have to look long and hard at the life of Jesus before assigning improbability to it.

The extraordinary post-resurrection encounters and appearances of Jesus provide the final line of proof. The New Testament states that nearly five hundred people saw Jesus alive and resurrected (1 Corinthians 15:6). This includes individuals such as the apostle Paul, who prior to his encounter with Christ had been the chief persecutor of Christians. Paul had absolutely no motivation to lay eyes on Jesus, so his experience cannot be reduced to hallucinatory wishful thinking. Furthermore, if anyone could have produced a body or a plausible reason why it was missing, or could have explained why so many people had seen Jesus, Christianity would have simply gone away. But no one could.

Christianity initially flourished in Jerusalem before seeping out to neighboring territories, and it is estimated that by the end of the first century nearly a million Jews had become followers of Christ. Many of these people had actually witnessed Jesus' life and ministry. They were zealously bound to their faith and culture, and yet broke from traditional Judaism to become followers of Christ. Clearly the amount of evidence for Jesus' resurrection, and the number of his post-resurrection appearances, must have been staggering to explain this.

The only alternative theory posed by Christianity's early opponents was that the disciples stole the body. So it might be worth considering the probability of this alternative. Obviously, if they had stolen the body, the disciple's actions, motivation and martyrdoms seem inexplicable— we've just covered that. As this was a Roman execution, a Roman guard of four to sixteen soldiers would have been placed at the tomb, and customarily a two-ton boulder would be rolled downhill to the mouth of the tomb. The Gospels mention that Jesus was laid in the tomb of Joseph of Arimathea, a member of the Sanhedrin, Israel's presidential cabinet, making Joseph a national celebrity. So there's no mistaking the facticity and location of his tomb. And in the wake of Jesus' sudden persecution, the disciples were all terrified, scattered and in hiding. So the disciples making off with the body remains highly problematic to say the least.[16]

So, from a historical perspective, we are looking at a cataclysmic effect on the world: an enormous dent in history. The question that most of these evidences pose is, does anything less than Jesus' resurrection suffice to explain the enormous wrinkle in time? Within the culture of Israel, all other possible reconstructions leave us with a Jesus who, historically speaking, is going nowhere. In a different place and time, this might not be the case, but within first-century, monotheistic Judaism, nothing short of a resurrected Messiah would have generated the observable aftershocks.[17]

The evidence seems to suggest that the resurrection is not only reasonable but probable. All evidence, that is, except for this: experience tells us that normal people do not rise from the dead. And that is really the question: was Jesus just a normal person? Once you've decided that, the question of the resurrection answers itself.

The Commissioning of the Disciples

The eleven disciples went to Galilee, to the mountain where Jesus had told them to go. When they saw him, they worshiped him; but some doubted. Then Jesus came to them and said, "All authority in heaven and on earth has been given to me. Therefore go and make disciples of all nations, baptizing them in the name of the Father and of the Son and of the Holy Spirit, and teaching them to obey everything I have commanded you. And surely I am with you always, to the very end of the age." (Matthew 28:16-20)

The last scene in a movie is pivotal because it brings closure to the story and provides an important bridge to any planned sequel. In the closing of *Spider-Man 2,* for example, Peter Parker's nemesis (a word always to be used when discussing superheroes), Harry Osborn, discovers his father's hidden Green Goblin paraphernalia: mask, tights, pantyhose, that kind of thing. As a result we expect the future to hold a "Curse of the Green Goblin" sort of sequel. The closing scene in the Gospels is Jesus' post-resurrection discourse. It's exceedingly crucial because, while it does bring closure to the ministry of Jesus, a sequel of sorts is indeed planned: the growth and mission of the apostolic church, which will occupy the rest of the New Testament. This discourse is the bridge to that sequel.

I can better explain the discourse if we start with the definition of the word *plot:* "a series of causally related events, involving some sort of conflict or tension, leading to a climax and a resolution." Think of the TV show *Lost,* for example. What was the plot? Getting off the island. The tension, conflict and movement of the story revolved around this objective.

The Old Testament, as a book, has a plot, and that plot is the expansion of God's reign on the earth, with the conflict being skirmishes against the powers of evil. Israel was the manifestation of God's reign and presence in the world, and from Israel, the kingdom of God was to expand to the nations, as the book of Genesis adumbrates: "I will make your descendants as numerous as the stars in the sky and will give them all these lands, and through your offspring all nations on earth will be blessed" (Genesis 26.4).

But here's the tension in the drama, indeed the tension of the Old Testament: as history unfolded, Israel vacillated in its role as ambassador of the kingdom. Will Israel be obedient to the covenant or fall into godless idolatry and immorality? Tune in next week to find out. Week after week, year after year, Israel lives out this recurring soap opera. But then, in a shocking turn of events, the nation of Israel rejected its Messiah and, at least for now, has been written out of the show. "Wait a second. Give me that script—this can't be true." But tragically, it is true.

And so we are left to wonder what will happen to the plot now that the star has left the set. Well, the end of the Gospels contain the new script. The plot is going to remain the same: the expansion of God's kingdom on earth, but with new actors (the church) and some interesting nuances in upcoming episodes.

In the new season, the geography of Israel loses its relevance; rather, the gospel message will be dispatched to all nations, with the new kingdom being comprised of people from every language and nation. It will not be a physical, geopolitical kingdom with castle, moat and border guards, but a spiritual kingdom, with Christ reigning in the hearts of individual followers. The temple in Jerusalem, as the dwelling place of God, becomes a billion living temples, as God's Spirit will personally indwell every believer. And in light of all this kingdom expansion, Christ's followers are told to "go," to take his message to everyone outside the kingdom, or anyone who has never heard, and proclaim it to them.

This passage, then, is the introduction and movie trailer for the rest of the New Testament, which follows the new script in its opening episodes. (I have grown so fond of this TV metaphor, I find myself unable to stop wielding it.) The disciples disperse, spreading the message of Christ in ever-widening circles, encompassing Judea, Samaria, Macedonia, Athens, Rome . . . The letters of the New Testament are simply that: letters written to groups of Christians (churches) in locations to which the disciples had traveled and preached, making disciples.

This is the plot of the present age, the trajectory of history, and this discourse also elucidates how long this present age will last: "And this gospel of the kingdom will be preached in the whole world as a testimony to all nations, and then the end will come" (Matthew 24:14).

Where we are in this plot depends on whom you ask. There has been a concerted effort and cooperation among all churches toward this end in the last century, and a reasonable estimate is that nearly 5 billion people on the planet have been exposed to the gospel of Jesus Christ, leaving roughly 2 billion still out of earshot. With communication what it is, it's hard for me to imagine anyone on the planet, by the end of the twenty-first century, not having their own cell phone, blog and liter of Coke. So it's probably not a stretch to presume that the next century will witness the conclusion of this exceedingly more sacred marketing task. I've written this book so you can't say I haven't done my part.

The Ascension of the Christ

He said to them, "This is what I told you while I was still with you: Everything must be fulfilled that is written about me in the Law of Moses, the Prophets and the Psalms."

Then he opened their minds so they could understand the Scriptures. He told them, "This is what is written: The Christ will suffer and rise from the dead on the third day, and repentance and forgiveness of sins will be preached in his name to all nations, beginning at Jerusalem. . . .

When he had led them out to the vicinity of Bethany, he lifted up his hands and blessed them. While he was blessing them, he left them and was taken up into heaven. Then they worshiped him and returned to Jerusalem with great joy. And they stayed continually at the temple, praising God. (Luke 24:44-53)

There is a standard formula to action film trailers. Starting slow, scenes blink in and out. The momentum builds as the music gets louder and the action faster, and as camera fades give way to jump-cuts. With your heart and adrenalin racing, the emotional roller coaster peaks at the top of the highest incline and pauses: no words, no scene cuts, no music, no anything. Then into that stillness is uttered the memorable line of the movie—"We traced the call. It's coming from inside the house." You know what's coming next. Your eyes will be force-fed a thousand frames of film a second, the music will shrill to a siren and the ride will crash into a black wall—"Coming this June."

For the disciples the pause has already come. Before Jesus ascends and "Coming Soon" fades onto the screen, they are going to have to digest every messianic scene of the Old Testament in a single sitting. And that is a considerable amount of footage. Spiritually speaking, everything that was Israel—the Law, the festivals, the sacrificial system, the Temple, the prophets, the sabbath—everything that was subsumed in the Old Testament found its fulfillment in the Christ. As the architect of the nation, God had designed it precisely this way. Israel was the keyhole to the kingdom, made to fit a very specific key.

For example, the Passover, like the Fourth of July, commemorated the birth of a nation. You may have a basic idea of the Passover plot: Israel is delivered from the land of Egypt. Judgment in the form of plagues roll through Egypt like hurricanes through Florida, and as the last and final plague—the plague of the firstborns—"passes through" Egypt, it miraculously "passes over" the Israelites. Specifically, it passes over only those houses whose doorposts have been marked with the blood of a spotless lamb (Exodus 12). We can almost hear Jesus asking the disciples rhetorically: "And why do you suppose God did that?" It's a picture or symbol: God's judgment is averted, and we are delivered, only through the sacrifice of a spotless (read *sinless*) lamb, God's own "firstborn." John the Baptist had pieced this much together the first time he laid eyes on Jesus: "Look, the Lamb of God, who takes away the sin of the world!" (John 1:29)

Or consider the Day of Atonement (Yom Kippur). Once a year the Jewish High Priest would put his hands on a spotless goat to symbolically transfer the sins of the people to the animal, and then slay it. The transference of guilt and judgment to an innocent sacrifice (or scapegoat) was the principle behind the entire Jewish sacrificial system. Did God delight in the death of innocent animals? No! The point of the sacrificial system was to prepare Israel for its coming Messiah, the ultimate sin-bearer.

The Temple, which was the center of Israel's worship and the place to which every Jew flocked for high holy days, was the symbol of the nation—the Capitol building, so to speak. Like any monument, its significance was not *that* it stood but *what* it stood *for:* God's unique dwelling place among people—God with us. The prophet Isaiah, however, clarifies that the Jerusalem Temple was nothing more than a Lego model of the real thing: the coming Messiah: "The virgin will be with child and will give birth to a son, and will call him Immanuel" (Isaiah 7:14). Why would the Messiah be called Immanuel, as opposed to, say, Seth or Kennedy? Because the name Immanuel means "God with us"; the name Kennedy means "misshapen head." Israel's deliverer would be the ultimate temple, the ultimate manifestation of God with us and among us.

And so the Temple, the Holy Days, festivals and sacrificial system all foreshadowed the Christ. The words of the prophets, too, find their translation only through the Messiah. At the heart of their preaching and predictions was a composite sketch of the coming Redeemer: a man born in Bethlehem (Micah 5:2), from the province of Galilee (Isaiah 9:1), conceived of a virgin (Isaiah 7:14), pierced for our transgressions (Psalm 22), and one who was not just a man but "God with us" (Isaiah 7:14).

These and dozens of other predictions provided a have-you-seen-this-man? description for all Israel to be on the lookout. The future-telling of the prophets find their fulfillment in Jesus and are, frankly, unintelligible apart from him.

And then there is the sabbath, the day of rest. "There remains, then, a Sabbath-rest for the people of God; for anyone who enters God's rest also rests from his own work" (Hebrews 4:9-10). In other words, the sabbath foretells of grace: a rest from the labor of earned righteousness and a reprieve from a 168-hour workweek demanded by an exacting taskmaster such as the Mosaic Law: "Christ is the end of the law so that there may be righteousness for everyone who believes" (Romans 10:4).

We could go on, and I'm guessing that Jesus did—for hours—showing how the "Law of Moses, the prophets and the psalms" were completely and totally about him. And then, having fulfilled the mission for which he came, Jesus left. Gone, as mysteriously and miraculously as he had arrived. The Gospels tell us that he was taken up into heaven, and there he remains until he comes again—returning not as humanity's convicted felon but as "judge [of] the living and the dead" (2 Timothy 4:1).

6 WHY

What Was the Point?

Having read through the Gospels, or at least my digestible version of them, you should have seen a clear message and mission emerging from the ministry of Jesus: redemption. I really believe this is the ultimate need, the deepest cry, of the human heart. (A craving for Doritos may also be universal, its triangular shape one of Plato's forms, but I'm less certain of this.) The stories, movies and songs that inspire and don't simply commiserate with the human condition speak to our longing for redemption. And therefore, with so much talk of redemption, perhaps we should define it. On second thought, no, an illustration would be better, for redemption is always linked to a story line.

In the movie *Cinderella Man,* Russell Crowe plays Jim Braddock, a boxer who through injury, bad breaks and the Great Depression finds himself in a life-and-death struggle to keep his family from submerging so far below the poverty line that they cease to exist as a family. They stoop so low, so eye level with the gutter, that Jim Braddock sells all he owns, surrenders his pride and begs enough money to keep his electricity on and his family together.

Upon reaching the bottom (which is the neighborhood where redemption lives), Braddock's former boxing manager offers him a fight and a stepladder out of misery. Braddock enters the ring as a changed man. He is reborn with purpose and motivation, able to break free from the gravity of failure. He fights his way to the heavyweight championship and is vindicated before the entire country—Jim Braddock is resurrected.

Scratch that. I think a better scene is in *Shawshank Redemption* when Tim Robbins (playing Andy Dufresne) emerges from a sewage pipe, allowing the rain of freedom to wash over and cleanse him. And redemption, of course, is never more powerful than when Morgan Freeman narrates it.

We could, in fact, list hundreds of movies and songs with the same theme, for as I said, it is pervasive to the point of being a myth or a Jungian type. It is the story we always hear and never tire of hearing. In the human equation, redemption is π.

Spiritual Redemption

While a prominent theme in and of itself, spiritual redemption does not tug at the heart the way its temporal sibling does, but that owes itself more to the illusion born out of movies than it does to reality.

Here's what I mean by that. In any Jim Braddock story, immediately after the temporal redemption has occurred, the camera stops filming: a gratifying moment of vindication before the credits roll. That's nice, as far as it goes. But in the real world, such redemption is always momentary—a snapshot—and life continues on after the climactic scene wraps. The love that brought temporal redemption grows cold, bitter or maybe just stagnant until it's just two octogenarians staring without conversation over black coffee at 11:00 a.m. in McDonald's. Or maybe there's an affair a decade later. Or one of the partners dies early, leaving the other in a nursing home for twenty years of loneliness. All vehicles of temporal redemption are themselves subject to decay.

Like many writers, I am subject to bouts of depression. During one of my extended wakes (depressions), I turned to tobacco. Thank God for tobacco, or whatever they lace it with, because it brought relief, parole from my darkened cell. Tobacco is the workingman's antidepressant. Some years later, though, a doctor's exam showed a precancerous growth, which led to the realization that the tobacco equation doesn't balance—the joy of smoking is never equivalent to the agony of quitting. The means of my temporary deliverance contained within itself the terminal seeds of cancer.

And so it is with all temporal means of redemption—a job, money, success, relationships. They tug us out of one tire rut, only to drag us into the other, for the camera of life is always rolling, always rolling.

Religion

It is the shortened life span of earthly redemption that leads most to their need for ultimate, or spiritual, redemption.

I just watched the movie *Aeon Flux* because, with the exception of *Kill Bill,* the film genre of fashion-model-as-psychotic-assassin had all but passed me by. Here is the *Aeon Flux* plot: People never really die: they are cloned. Death is a commercial break between reruns. But the movie has a happy ending: a cure is found, the practice of perpetual cloning is brought to an end, and people can once again return to the "hope" of death, not having to contend with the wearisome aspects of continued existence.

I'm not sure what philosophy student wrote the screenplay for *Aeon Flux,* but I assure you that the prospect of nonexistence is not a comforting thought to those on their deathbed. It is only comforting in the abstract, and if there is one thing a deathbed is not, it is abstract. And it is for this reason that most people eventually seek out spiritual redemption.

But where does one go for spiritual redemption? Usually to one of the major religions, unless you're really wealthy; then you can create your own.

What one finds in religion, though, is not redemption but the *possibility* or *path* to redemption. Certain activities are required, and if you choose an Eastern version, certain lifetimes are required. But that which we seek— acceptance before God—is elusive. Have we done enough? What is the criterion or cut-off point? What if we're one good deed short? Will a pilgrimage be required? Have we arrived? The result is that religion infuses us with guilt—there must be some commandment we're in the process of breaking—and our guilt is assuaged only by judging others, for if someone is morally beneath us, we must be closer to the top, closer to redemption.

It's like we are on one side of a canyon and God is on the other, and we are constantly building bridges to get to the other side, only to find that whatever bridge we have chosen—philosophy, religion, social justice—cannot possibly span the distance.

Grace

Then into the universe enters grace: true redemption and not simply the promise of it. In Jesus Christ, God does for us what we could never do for ourselves—dying for our sins and applying to us his perfect life—and that is as close to a definition for *grace* as we're ever likely to find. Our part of redemption is making a decision to humble ourselves and accept God's hand out of the mire, to place faith in Jesus Christ, to consent to be redeemed.

I'm not sure there is any one way to do that. As in a marriage, there's any number of ways to say your vows. I eloped, so I wouldn't really know. I simply said "I do" to a justice of the peace, and that was it. I believe that's about all I said to God too. As a freshman in college, lying in my bed, reading one of those green Gideon Bibles people give you, I said "I do" to Christ. Actually, what I said was something like "Jesus, I want to know you. I want you to forgive my sins. I want you to change and direct my life. I want eternal life, and I believe you can do all of these things—

that you *will* do all of these things."

A simple prayer, followed by redemption. And as you've probably figured out already, it was that change in my life that has animated this book. As a recipient of grace, I feel somewhat constrained to explain it to others, to explain it to *you*. If redemption is what you really seek, then simply express that to God in your own words—or feel free to use mine.

Some entrepreneurial states still offer you money for your aluminum cans. You take your empty Fresca six-packs to a redemption center, and they'll give you money—nice, shiny money. This is as it should be. This is the theology of redemption. The moment you make that decision, the moment you say "I do," Christ takes your sin and credits you with his righteousness. Not the hope of redemption. Redemption.

> I tell you the truth, whoever hears my word and believes him who sent me has eternal life and will not be condemned; he has crossed over from death to life. (John 5:24)

So . . . Do you?

APPENDIX

Questions About the New Testament

A study of the Gospels raises questions concerning the New Testament itself: Who wrote it? When? How was it compiled? How can I get some of my own short stories included in it? Recent books such as *The Da Vinci Code* have also raised questions along these lines. This appendix is not meant to be exhaustive but to address some of the most common questions concerning the New Testament. For further study I'd recommend *The Canon of Scripture* by F. F. Bruce (InterVarsity).

When were the books of the New Testament written?

Here's an important fact to keep in mind: Jesus died in roughly A.D. 30 to 33, not the year 0, because A.D. does not mean "After Death" but *anno Domini* ("in the year of our Lord").

With A.D. 30 as ground zero, most scholars date Paul's letters between A.D. 50 and 66, the first three Gospels between A.D. 50 and 70, and John's writings sometime between A.D. 80 and 90. That makes the majority of the epistles and three of the Gospels dated only twenty to forty years after the death of Jesus.

This, as Wikipedia would say, is the "scholarly consensus," and it's based on solid evidence. For example, writing in roughly A.D. 90, the bishop of Rome, Clement, quoted from many of the New Testament books, thus assuring that their dates are earlier than A.D. 90. Furthermore, by A.D. 110 to 120, a collection of Paul's letters had been gathered, bound and circulated to various churches. We actually have a manuscript of this collection, called the Beatty manuscript. This collection contains ten of Paul's thirteen letters found in the New Testament.

Yet even against such evidence there are scholars who push for later dates on several of the letters, and the reason is a simple presupposition. I'll try to illustrate.

When I go to McDonald's, I feel unhealthy even if I eat the McSalad. The reason is that I have a presupposition that McDonald's food can't be good for me. Even if the friendly cashier had hand-picked the lettuce and killed the cow herself, I would believe nothing to the contrary.

The skeptic's presupposition is a little more logical. It is the belief that the miraculous stories about Jesus (being born of a virgin, giving sight to the blind, and so on) couldn't possibly be true. Therefore, you can't have documents within the immediate generation after Jesus containing these ideas, because time would need to elapse for such myths to develop. Make sense?

Following from that presupposition, that Jesus was just an ordinary man, you simply must stretch out the time line for people believably to be referring to him as the sinless Son of God. If, on the other hand, the New Testament claims about Jesus are true, such dating gymnastics aren't necessary. But that said, there are certain books, such as Romans, Corinthians and Galatians, for which virtually no one would dispute an A.D. 50–60 dating.

Do we have any of the original New Testament documents?

No, but biblical scholars are constantly monitoring *Antiques Roadshow* in case one should emerge from an old shoebox in someone's attic.

So, how do we know our New Testament is accurate?

To evaluate the accuracy of our New Testament, we have to look at two factors. One factor is the number of ancient manuscripts (copies of the original) we possess, and the second is the time gap between when the original document was written and when the earliest surviving copies were written. The more manuscripts we have, and the closer the manuscripts are to the original, the better we are able to determine accuracy.

For example, we have seven manuscript copies of *Natural History,* written by Pliny Secundus, with a 750-year gap between the earliest copy and the original text. The number-two book in all of history in manuscript authority is *The Iliad,* written by Homer, for which we have 643 copies with a 400-year gap.[1]

Now, this is a little startling. We currently have 24,970 manuscript copies of the New Testament, completely towering over all other works of antiquity in documentary evidence. In addition, we have one fragment of the New Testament (NT) with only a 50-year gap from when the original was written, whole books with only a 100-year gap, and the whole NT with only a 225- to 250-year gap.[2] Given the number of early copies, there is no question that we know what the original documents said, though see my note below.

(Occasionally a word can vary among ancient manuscripts, as they were hand copied and not xeroxed. When this happens the variant word with the greater amount of manuscript attestation [900 manuscripts said 'hare' vs. 3 that said 'hair] is chosen for the translation. On the rare occasion where a decision is difficult, you'll find the two variations noted in the margin of your Bible, neither of which will obscure the basic meaning of the passage.)

What role did Constantine and the Council of Nicea play in deciding what would go in the New Testament?

Dan Brown's *The Da Vinci Code* makes some creative statements concerning the New Testament, which can be disconcerting to those who are not familiar with church history (and perhaps even more disconcerting to those who are). Constantine had nothing to do with deciding on the books of the New Testament. Of the twenty rulings made at the Council of Nicea (A.D. 325), none dealt with the contents of the New Testament. Constantine convened the council to provide spiritual unity and a clear church position on an ongoing debate causing division within the newly Christianized Roman Empire. That debate was not about the New Testament but about the nature of Christ.

Specifically, the debate was about whether Jesus was coeternal with the Father, that is, if there was a time in eternity past when Jesus "was not." No one at the council thought Jesus was just a man or a prophet. The debate was concluded with a 300-to-2 vote deciding that Jesus was coeternal with the Father. Thus the Nicene Creed affirms that Jesus was "one in being with the Father, begotten not made."[3]

When was the New Testament decided upon?

Most of the letters and Gospels of the New Testament were recognized as Scripture before the end of the first century. Yet, as letters, these documents circulated in various geographic regions, and so it is closer to about A.D. 150 (175 years prior to Nicea) before we have a comprehensive list that closely reflects our New Testament.

Without going into elaborate documentation, we (my laptop and I) will simply note that the church leader Irenaeus, writing in approximately A.D. 180, attested to the universally held scriptural status of the four Gospels, Acts, Romans, 1 and 2 Corinthians, Galatians, Ephesians, Philippians, Colossians, 1 and 2 Thessalonians, 1 and 2 Timothy, Titus, 1 Peter, 1 John, and Revelation. That's most of our New Testament.[4]

In fact, the general contents of the New Testament were so well established that the church felt no need to formalize the list until heresy, forgeries, missions and other factors of the third and fourth centuries necessitated a New Testament list that would forever be unaltered.

And so, at the synod of Hippo (A.D. 393), not at Nicea, the church listed the twenty-seven confirmed books of the New Testament. This was not a creative brainstorm but a ratification of what the church had held to be true for more than two and half centuries.

How did the church come to recognize the books of the New Testament as Scripture?

There were four major criteria. The first is fairly obvious: was it written by one of the disciples? While most of the authors, such as Peter and John, were clearly disciples, what about Mark and Luke, whom we didn't see sitting at the Last Supper? Early Christian writings explain why these books were included.

- "Mark, the disciple and interpreter of Peter, did also hand down to us in writing what had been preached by Peter." (Papias, A.D. 60–140)[5]

- "Luke also, the companion of Paul, recorded in a book the Gospel preached by him." (Irenaeus, A.D. 120–200)[6]

The second criterion was, did the writing conform to the doctrine that had been handed down from the original disciples to their disciples and so on? Third, did the document have wide use and attestation from the earliest and most recognized churches (usually those founded by the disciples) and church leaders? Last, the testimony of the disciples of the original disciples were taken into account, considering what was said by those who had lived on into the second century and testified to their first-hand knowledge of what were authentic apostolic documents. Papias, for example, mentioned his acquaintance with many who had been personally taught by the disciples.[7]

Were there other gospels not included in the New Testament, and if so, why were they excluded?

We know of roughly sixty other documents, most of them not Gospels, that can be traced to several of the predominant cults of the second and third century, mainly the Gnostics. These documents were almost all written well into the second century, bearing the pseudonyms of the apostles. Our copies of many of these works came from the discovery of an ancient Gnostic library (Nag Hammadi) in 1945.

The earliest of these "alternative gospels" actually exaggerate Christ's deity, attempting to deny his humanity, as the Gnostics held that matter (flesh) was evil and that it was therefore inconceivable that Jesus could have been an actual man. The documents were far from secret. The early Christians were aware of both the cults and their writings and went to great length to condemn and combat them. You might want to read the early work *Against Heresies,* written by the noted church leader Irenaeus (A.D. 120–200). The book records the names of several of these works and pseudo-gospels, citing from which cult they emanated and defending what Christians from the very beginning believed about these doctrines.

The Marriage of Jesus and Mary?

While the Gospels do lack romance and a love interest, not a single ancient source indicates that Jesus was married, let alone to Mary Magdalene. By ancient sources, I mean the writings of the New Testament, the writings of early Christians and church leaders, and even the writings of second-century cults such as the Gnostics. The Gospel of the Nazarenes, the Gospel of the Egyptians, the Gospel of the Ebionites, the Gospel of Mary, the Gospel of Peter—not a mention in any of these Gnostic documents. Simply put, there is no historical basis for the claim, and no reputable New Testament scholar would say otherwise.

While it is clear that the apostle Paul, John the Baptist and Jesus were all single, the apostle Paul indicated that many of the disciples had wives ("Don't we have the right to take a believing wife along with us, as do the other apostles and the Lord's brothers and Cephas?" [1 Corinthians 9:5]). And, as marriage is clearly not a sin, it is inexplicable why all of the ancient sources would indicate that these three were unmarried, unless they were.

As for the idea that Jesus had a child and that there was a royal bloodline, how should I explain this? Besides there being no mention in human history of a royal bloodline coming from Jesus, the very idea of it misunderstands the nature of the kingdom of God, making it an earthly one with actual royalty. Hopefully this book, and a more informed understanding of the Gospels, will have disabused anyone of such a misunderstanding of the kingdom that Jesus preached.

Understanding Biblical Prophecy

The Old Testament contains sixty-one specific prophecies and nearly three hundred references to the future Messiah. Within this book we looked at only about six or seven of the most specific: the virgin birth, Bethlehem, the crucifixion and whatever else I wrote.

When one looks at the prophecies in their biblical context they are faced with some puzzling issues: the prophecies, in their context, seem to relate more to events in the immediate future and the particular situation faced by the Old Testament prophet. They are not clearly highlighted with introductory phrases like, "At this point I'm going to speak to you about the coming Messiah." Events in the immediate future bleed into events in the far future without any clear demarcation within the prophecy.

An entire book—a book I have no desire to write—could be devoted to the many nuances and literary features of biblical prophecy. But let me at least provide some basic categories and interpretive clues that you may find useful.

Clear Messianic Texts

There are certain Old Testament prophecies that come in a form you would have eagerly hoped for: clear statements by the prophets that leave little room for confusion concerning the coming Messiah. A prophecy like Micah's (700 B.C.) could fall into this camp:

> You, Bethlehem Ephrathah,
>   though you are small among the clans of Judah,
> out of you will come for me
>   one who will be ruler over Israel,
> whose origins are from of old,
>   from ancient times. (Micah 5:2)

There just isn't a whole lot of ambiguity of what, and who, Micah is talking about, and for that we shall always love him.

Telescoping

"The Lord himself will give you a sign: The virgin will be with child and will give birth to a son, and will call him Immanuel" (Isaiah 7:14)

Like many messianic prophecies, Isaiah's prediction (seventh century B.C.) dealt with a specific and immediate situation in his day. Ahaz, the king of Judah, was terrified of an impending attack. To keep the king from losing heart, Isaiah went to him and provided some divine perspective on the situation. And, as a sign that his words were from God, Isaiah told Ahaz something to the effect of, "Look, there's a specific, unmarried woman that you know, and that everyone knows will never be married or have children. But when she does have children it will be a sign that everything I said to you was from God."

The text goes on to say that the child will be called "Immanuel," a name that means "God with us." In fact, in Isaiah 9 the further description of the child states:

He will be called

Wonderful Counselor, Mighty God,

Everlasting Father, Prince of Peace.

Of the increase of his government and peace

there will be no end. (Isaiah 9:6, 7)

These descriptions make it clear that the prophecy had a second, more ultimate fulfillment in the coming of the Messiah. In fact, by around the third century B.C., Jewish writings and interpretation concerning this passage affirmed its messianic understanding and the expectancy of a virgin birth as a "sign" of the coming Messiah.[8]

Now, besides the messianic language describing the child, what helped the Jewish interpreters figure this out was a well-known and prominent feature of biblical prophecy called "telescoping." Telescoping is where the immediate future and messianic future merge together like the tops of two hills on the horizon. It's really not brain surgery; it occurs so often in the Old Testament you just begin to recognize it when you see it.

Telescoping was based on what we'll call the "two age" principle. In the prophetic world there were really only two time zones: this age (today) and the messianic age. So Old Testament prophecy, generally speaking, see-saws from the present to the messianic age—there and back, there and back, there and back. So if the prophet isn't talking about his current situation, he's generally talking about the messianic age. That simple.

However, since the coming of Christ, Christians read Old Testament prophecy with a slightly different perspective, seeing three mountain-tops, or ages, instead of two. In other words, some aspect of prophecy dealt with the prophet's immediate time frame, some aspect referred to the first coming of Christ (his suffering and death), and a third aspect refers to the second coming of Christ.

Ok, so let's pretend we're Isaiah and write a sample prophecy, "I see the Babylonian army coming to annihilate us; no, wait, there's a suffering servant riding the lead horse wearing a crown of thorns, but in the distance I see one like the Son of Man, coming on the clouds, and the end of suffering forevermore." See how easy that was?

Types

Not wanting to add further complexity to the book, I chose not to touch on biblical types, of which there are literally countless examples. A type is an event or circumstance that bears an uncanny similarity to something yet to happen. It's like the foreshadowing an author might use within a novel to anticipate the climax or a key event in the story. God, being an absolute genius, can foreshadow in history, in geography and in the lives of men and women. The Old Testament is filled with these echoes of sounds that haven't yet occurred, pictures that became recognizable after Christ appeared. Let's take a look at one.[9]

Shortly after their exodus out of Egypt, the Israelites, as punishment for disobedience, were overrun with venomous snakes. When the people repented, God provided a remedy to the problem.

> The people came to Moses and said, "We sinned when we spoke against the LORD and against you. Pray that the LORD will take the snakes away from us." So Moses prayed for the people.
>
> The LORD said to Moses, "Make a snake and put it up on a pole; anyone who is bitten can look at it and live." So Moses made a bronze snake and put it up on a pole. Then when anyone was bitten by a snake and looked at the bronze snake, he lived. (Numbers 21:7-9)

Now fast-forward about fourteen hundred years, to a conversation Jesus had with a Jewish leader named Nicodemus:

> No one has ever gone into heaven except the one who came from
> heaven—the Son of Man. Just as Moses lifted up the snake in the
> desert, so the Son of Man must be lifted up, that everyone who be-
> lieves in him may have eternal life. (John 3:13-15)

Did you catch it? It wasn't a prophecy but a type: a historical event, place or person that foreshadows the coming Messiah. Jesus declared this exodus event to be a case of divine foreshadowing: something God did in history whose ultimate meaning or significance became clear in and through his life. The Old Testament is saturated with such types.

In recognizing these prophetic features I think you'll begin to see just how much of the Old Testament pointed to Christ, and how little of it is comprehensible without him.

Acknowledgments

For the completion of this work I am indebted to many and to Katie, my wife, to whom I owe all things.

The book is first and foremost owing to the editorial excellence of David Zimmerman, who streamlined and structured a very long and meandering stackage of words.

It is published due, and only due, to the prompting, aid and encouragement of Eric Stanford.

And it is greatly beholding to the refining thoughts of Will Walker and Brett Westervelt, the literary wisdom of Katie James, the close reads of Tanya Walker and the theological scrutiny of Byron Straughn.

Lastly, it is the result of encouragement provided by Tim Henderson, Mike Sorgius, Larry Stephens, Mark Gauthier and Mat Weiss, and the friendship of Keith Davy.

To all of you, thank you.

NOTES

Chapter One: Contact

[1]Flavius Josephus, *Antiquities of the Jews* (Peabody, Mass.: Hendrickson, 1987), pp. 63-64.

[2]Quoted in Ravi Zacharias, *Just Thinking* <www.rzim.org>, winter 1998.

[3]Rabbi Shimeon Ben Azzai, Yeb. IV 3; 49a.

[4]Quoted in Ben Witherington III, "Birth of Jesus," in *Dictionary of Jesus and the Gospels,* ed. Joel B. Green, Scot McKnight and I. Howard Marshall (Downers Grove, Ill.: InterVarsity Press, 1992), pp. 72-73.

[5]Nostradamus, *The Nostradamus Encyclopedia,* ed. Peter Lemesurier (New York: St. Martin's Press, 1997), pp. 138-39.

[6]Peter W. Stoner, *Science Speaks* (Chicago: Moody Press, 1958), pp. 97-110. Stoner's work was reviewed by the American Scientific Affiliation, which stated, "The mathematical analysis . . . is based upon principles of probability which are thoroughly sound, and Professor Stoner has applied these principles in a proper and convincing way" (quoted on p. 5).

[7]Thomas Hock, trans., *Infancy Gospel of Thomas* (Santa Rosa, Calif.: Polebridge, 1996), pp. 1-4.

[8]Irenaeus *Against Heresies.* I might have added "four like the number of paws on an otter" or "four like the number of Junior Mints contained in a box marked 'king-sized,'" but these were serious times and serious people.

[9]Josephus, *Antiquities,* pp. 116-19.

Chapter Two: Vulgar

[1]Example from Darrell Bock in *Jesus Under Fire* (Grand Rapids: Zondervan, 1995), pp. 74-99.

[2]Bono, quoted in Michka Assayas, *Bono: In Conversation with Michka Assayas* (New York: Riverhead, 2005).

[3]Quoted in Peter Kreeft and Ronald K. Tacelli, *Handbook of Christian Apologetics* (Downers Grove, Ill.: InterVarsity Press, 1993), p. 150.

[4]C. S. Lewis, *Mere Christianity* (San Francisco: HarperCollins, 1972), p. 51.

Chapter Three: Marvel

[1]Paul Eshleman, *The Touch of Jesus* (Orlando: New Life Publications, 1985), p. 130.

²Thomas Allen, *Possessed* (Lincoln, Neb.: iUniverse, 2005), p. 243.

³Malachi Martin, *Hostage to the Devil* (San Francisco: HarperSanFrancisco, 1992), pp. 9-26.

⁴M. Scott Peck, *Glimpses of the Devil* (New York: Free Press, 2005).

⁵Concept taken from Gregory A. Boyd, *God at War* (Downers Grove, Ill.: InterVarsity Press, 1997), p. 41.

⁶Rikki Watts, *Isaiah's New Exodus in Mark* (Grand Rapids: Baker, 2000), p. 30.

Chapter Four: Scandalon

¹Wikipedia, "Every Breath You Take," accessed online at <http://en.wikipedia.org/wiki/Every_Breath_You_Take>.

²Chandler Burr, *The Emperor of Scent* (New York: Random House, 2002), pp. 96-97.

³John Stott, *The Cross of Christ* (Downers Grove, Ill.: InterVarsity Press, 1986), p. 108.

⁴Peter Kreeft, *Making Sense Out of Suffering* (Ann Arbor, Mich.: Servant, 1986), p. 130.

⁵C. S. Lewis, *The Problem of Pain* (New York: Macmillan, 1962), p. 119.

⁶Ibid., p. 127.

⁷Ibid., p. 125.

⁸Timothy George, *Theology of the Reformers* (Nashville: Broadman, 1992), p. 48.

Chapter Five: Scapegoat

¹Paul M. Maier, *Pontius Pilate* (Garden City, N.Y.: Doubleday, 1968).

²John McRay, *Archaeology and the New Testament* (Grand Rapids: Baker, 1991), p. 227.

³Norman Geisler, *Baker Encyclopedia of Apologetics* (Grand Rapids: Baker, 1999), p. 47.

⁴J. A. Thompson, *The Bible and Archaeology,* 3rd ed. (Grand Rapids: Eerdmans, 1982), pp. 414-15.

⁵Geisler, *Baker Encyclopedia,* p. 47.

⁶Murray J. Harris, *The Second Epistle to the Corinthians,* New International Greek Testament Commentary (Grand Rapids: Eerdmans, 2005), p. 185.

⁷Paul W. Barnett, *Jesus and the Logic of History* (Downers Grove, Ill.: InterVarsity Press, 1997), pp. 84-89.

⁸Lucian, *The Passing of Peregrinus* (Cambridge, Mass.: Harvard University Press, 1936), pp. 13, 15.

⁹Flavius Josephus, *Antiquities of the Jews* (Peabody, Mass.: Hendrickson, 1987), pp. 63-64.

¹⁰Tacitus, *Annals* (New York: Oxford University Press, 2000), 15.44.

¹¹Quoted in Josh McDowell, *The New Evidence That Demands a Verdict* (San Bernardino, Calif.: Here's Life, 1999), p. 224.

¹²Larry Chapman, *Y-Jesus* (Orlando: Bright Media, 2004).

¹³Peter Steinfels, "Jesus Died—and Then What Happened?" *New York Times,* April 3, 1988, E9.

¹⁴Josh McDowell, *More Than a Carpenter* (Wheaton, Ill.: Living Books, 1977), p. 61.

¹⁵J. P. Moreland, *Scaling the Secular City* (Grand Rapids: Baker, 1987), pp. 160-83.

¹⁶Josh McDowell, *A Ready Defense* (San Bernardino, Calif.: Here's Life, 1990), pp. 221-35.

[17]Barnett, *Jesus and the Logic of History,* p. 34.

Appendix

[1]Josh McDowell, *The New Evidence That Demands a Verdict* (San Bernardino, Calif.: Here's Life, 1999), p. 42.

[2]Ibid., p. 40.

[3]Darrell L. Bock, *Breaking the Da Vinci Code* (Nashville: Thomas Nelson, 2006).

[4]New Testament books referenced throughout Irenaeus, *St. Irenaeus of Lyons, Book 1: Against the Heresies,* trans. Dominic Unger (Paramus, N.J.: Newman, 1991).

[5]Eusebius *Historia Ecclesiastica* (Oxford: Oxford University Press, 1999), 3.39.15.

[6]Irenaeus *Against the Heresies* 3.1.1.

[7]Eusebius *Historia Ecclesiastica* 3.39.4.

[8]J. A. Motyer, "Context and Content in the Interpretation of Isaiah 7:14," *Tyndale Bulletin* 21 (1970): 118-25; Donald A. Hagner, *Word Biblical Commentary: Matthew 1-13* (Dallas: Word, 1993), pp. 20-21.

[9]Quoted from lecture given by Timothy Henderson in Washington, D.C., 2001.

Suggested Reading

Christ and Christianity

Chesterton, G. K. *Orthodoxy*. Mineola, N.Y.: Dover, 2004.
Eldredge, John. *Epic*. Nashville: Thomas Nelson, 2004.
Lewis, C. S. *Mere Christianity*. Grand Rapids: Zondervan, 2001.
Strobel, Lee. *The Case for Christ*. Grand Rapids: Zondervan, 2001.
———. *The Case for Faith*. Grand Rapids: Zondervan, 2000.

The New Testament

Bruce, F. F. *The Canon of Scripture*. Downers Grove, Ill.: InterVarsity Press, 1988.
———. *The Origin of the Bible*. Wheaton, Ill.: Tyndale House, 2004.
Carson, D. A. *Introduction to the New Testament*. Grand Rapids: Zondervan, 2002.
Geisler, Norman. *From God to Us*. Chicago: Moody Press, 1974.

For a safe place to explore issues about college, life and
what it might be like to know God, visit

everystudent.com

To order copies of *Jesus Without Religion*
for your friends, visit the book page at

ivpress.com

IF YOU LIKED THIS BOOK,
CONSIDER THESE OTHERS
FROM LIKEWISE

TRUE STORY
A Christianity Worth Believing In
by James Choung

Meet disillusioned believer Caleb
and hostile skeptic Anna. They're
on a journey of discovery about
what Jesus really came to do and
what Christianity is supposed to
be about.
978-0-8308-3609-3

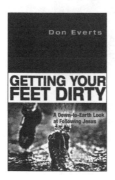

GETTING YOUR FEET DIRTY
*A Down-to-Earth Look
at Following Jesus*
by Don Everts

What's it like to start
following Jesus? What
comes next? This book
sets the scene.
978-0-8308-3604-8

FOR MORE BOOKS YOU MIGHT LIKE, VISIT
likewisebooks.com

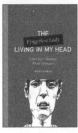